⤺·THE·⤻
ROYAL ANIMALS

THE ROYAL ANIMALS

Michele Brown

W. H. ALLEN · LONDON
A Howard & Wyndham Company
1981

This book or parts thereof may not be reproduced
in any form whatsoever without permission in writing

Printed and bound by L.E.G.O. Vicenza, Italy
for the publishers W H Allen & Co Ltd
44 Hill Street, London W1X 8LB

ISBN 0 491 02913 6

CONTENTS

On a bright summer day in 1941 the Princesses sit with one of their pets in the grounds of Windsor Castle

INTRODUCTION

*I*f Queen Elizabeth II had a fairy god-mother who could make all her wishes come true, or if it were possible to turn the clock back fifty years and change the course of history, the chances are that the Duchess of Edinburgh would be living the life of a country lady surrounded by 'lots of dogs and horses' — the sort of life which lies ahead of Princess Anne.

Yet in spite of the demands made on her by royal duties, the Queen still manages to slip away to the countryside in Norfolk and Scotland where she feels most at home. There she is free to trudge over ploughed fields with faithful, muddy, labradors or to ride over the lovely moorland country surrounding Balmoral on a favourite horse. At Sandringham, Balmoral and Windsor, she and her family can live the same life as their closest friends — the life of a well-to-do country family; a life which revolves around early morning gallops, week-end shooting parties and trips to the races.

However, like every other country family with a love of animals, the range of four-footed companions is not restricted to horses and dogs. There are children's pets, farm animals and race horses which all demand, and receive, their owners' constant interest and attention.

In the case of the royal family, however, the attention is not limited to the immediate family and their friends, it is a topic of fascination and appeal to the whole nation.

Today millions of us devote hours to feeding, grooming, exercising and occasionally rescuing our pets. We tolerate them when they are naughty and we dote on them when they behave as we expect them to — they are an abiding interest and we love them for it.

Admittedly, few of us have the means or resources to maintain a string of polo ponies or a couple of racing stables. Fewer still can afford to run half a dozen farms and shoot over the finest grouse moor and pheasant drives in the country, but we can, and do, identify with the truculent corgi that happily gets out of hand and suddenly lunges at the ankles of an important guest. Those of us who exhibit our own pets at dog shows and other competitions can imagine the sense of pride felt by the Queen Mother when her champion North Country Cheviot ram wins first prize at the Royal Highland Show. And when the Queen's horse gallops home ahead of the rest of the field at Longchamps or Chantilly, there are few of us who do not share a sense of national pride when we see the diminutive figure leading her horse into the winner's enclosure.

The British are a nation of animal lovers and for all the carping criticism about the Civil List, they are staunch supporters of their royal family — the combination of the two is unbeatable. Whether it is Prince Charles thundering over Smith's Lawn on a sweating polo pony, or Prince Philip fearlessly driving a team of horses through a muddy ford, or Princess Anne negotiating an impossible looking hurdle at Badminton, the British press are there to record the event and the British public love it.

The royal family essentially stands for tradition, and one of those traditions is a continuity of interest which stretches back almost one thousand years. There have been few kings and queens who have not owned favourite pets or sporting animals, and few

Above *Charles rides with his sister in Windsor Great Park 1969*

Left *The Queen Mother sits with one of her corgis, Royal Lodge, Windsor 1940*

Opposite above *A royal trumpet for the Queen at the Children's Party, Hyde Park 1979*

Opposite below *Anne and Mark appear together following the announcement of their engagement - naturally the dog gets in the picture too!*

who have not furthered the cause of their particular interest in one way or another.

Charles II laid the foundations for racing as we know it today. George III was an important figure in the development of British agriculture. Queen Victoria introduced many of our most popular breeds of

dogs into the country. And the legacy stretches back even further to the Plantagenet kings who ruled both England and France in the Middle Ages.

From King Harold and his falcons to Peter Phillips and the livestock of the Gatcombe estate, the royal families of Britain have been in the forefront of the national interest in, and obsession with, animals. And the fascination that the British public holds for its present royal family and the animals they have gathered around them is more than a common bond of interest — it is a link with the past and their whole national heritage.

ROYAL PETS

*F*or over forty years the short-legged, fox-faced and often irritable Welsh corgi has been virtually a trade mark of the royal family. In recent years the faithful, trusting labrador has joined him in convincing the English people that above all else their royal family is definitely a doggie family.

There is nothing new in this obvious royal predilection for dogs. Kings and Queens as far back as the eleventh century gave dogs pride of place and the English were probably a nation of dog lovers long before they were even unified under one crown.

In her great interest in dogs Her Majesty the Queen is following a long tradition which binds her to the affections and fellow interests of so many of her subjects. And perhaps today more than any time in history their genuine interest in, and love of, pets is the one great common factor that links the royal family with the rest of us.

William the Conqueror has become notorious for the forest laws imposed ruthlessly on the serfs who inhabited his royal hunting grounds. It is surprising to learn therefore that during the time of his successors, these laws were relaxed somewhat — not to favour the two-legged inhabitants of the forests, but the smaller four-footed ones. Although the presence of large dogs was still prohibited in the royal hunting reserves, smaller dogs, provided that they could fit through a special gauge that measured seven inches by five in diameter, were allowed to run free with few restrictions governing their behaviour.

The Plantagenet kings were also quick to appreciate the value of the dog as man's best friend. During the troubled reign of Henry III, the King sent for Master Williams, a monk at Westminster who had gained a reputation as something of a painter. He asked him to paint a picture of a king being rescued by his dogs from an attack made upon him by his subjects. The finished painting was hung in what then served as the King's 'bathroom', presumably as daily reminder that though the country might be in turmoil, he could always find support in the royal kennels.

Similarly the desertion of a favourite dog must have been a damning blow to any man's self esteem, and if that man was a king as well, the dog's action carried even greater significance. This was certainly the case with Richard II whose favourite greyhound, Mathe, inexplicably swapped its allegiance from Richard to none other than his rival and subsequent usurper, Henry Bolingbroke.

It was common knowledge that Mathe followed no one but the King; the hound would rush to greet his master, jumping up and placing his two front paws on Richard's shoulders. However, on the eve of Richard's last journey to London, when he and Bolingbroke were talking together in Flint Castle, Mathe was released to greet the King. But instead of throwing himself at Richard, as he always had done, the dog made straight for Bolingbroke and never left his side after that day. Richard's fate was sealed, and he, like Mathe, knew it.

Other royal dogs were, fortunately for their owners, either less perceptive or more blind in their devotion than Mathe. On the morning of 8 February 1586 Mary Queen of Scots was led into the great hall of Fotheringay to face her execution. In the tension of the moment no one noticed the faithful little spaniel that lovingly followed its mistress to the block until, as the official recorder notes, one of the executioners:

'. . . espied her little dogge which was crept under her clothes and could not be gotten forth but with force and afterwards would not depart from her dead corpse but came and lay between her head and shoulders.'

Sixty-three years later Mary's grandson, Charles I, was also followed to his execution by his pet spaniel Rogue. Rogue, however, did not stay to see his master's end due to the action of a die-hard Roundhead, Francis Tench.

Having failed to provoke the king with jeers and taunts while he walked to the scaffold at Whitehall, Tench grabbed the royal pet and carried it home with him, where he kept the poor animal chained in his cellar as a surrogate royal captive. Tench may have failed to anger Charles I, but theft of the dog greatly angered his eldest son. Within three months of the restoration a warrant had been issued for Tench's arrest but, no doubt to the new monarch's annoyance, nothing more was

heard of the thief.

As a dynasty the Stuarts were passionately devoted to dogs. Shortly after his arrival in England James I wrote to the Earl of Mar about:

'Some of these small dogges they call Terriers and in Scotland earth dogges, which are bothe stoute, good for killers and will stay longe in the grunde.'

The dogs King James was enquiring about were ancestors of one of the most popular breeds today, the cairn terrier, and he was probably the first person ever to bring them into England.

Like many hunting kings James had his favourite hounds, and of these the one he cherished most was Jowler. An amusing story is told concerning Jowler which provides an interesting insight into his masters's temperament.

The King and his followers had been hunting in Hertfordshire for some time, when one day His Majesty noticed after their return from a day in the field that Jowler was miss-

Far left *Queen Victoria with her dog Sharp, around 1868*

Left *In this piece of Roundhead propaganda Prince Rupert's white poodle, Boye, is mysteriously transformed into a black hell hound*

Above *A far more affectionate tribute is offered to the Queen's dead pets. Here are their gravestones at Sandringham*

ing. Fortunately, the hound reappeared the next day, bearing a note from some of the landlords who were reluctantly acting as hosts to the royal party.

'Good Mr. Jowler,' the note read, *'we pray you speak to the King (for he hears you every day and so he doth not us) that it please his Majesty to go back to London, for else the country will be undone; all our provision is spent and we are not able to entertain him any longer.'*

James read the message, found it highly amusing and carried on hunting in the area for another two weeks.

Jowler came to a sad end when James's wife, Queen Anne of Denmark, inadvertently hit him with a bolt from her cross-bow. Her husband was mortified and for some time the identity of the assassin was kept from him. When he eventually found out who had been responsible, he begged her forgiveness and sent her a costly present 'pretending it was a legacy from his dear dead dog.'

James's grandson Prince Rupert inherited his grandfather's love of dogs from his mother Princess Elizabeth. During his three year imprisonment at Linz in Austria, he was given a white poodle to keep him company. He named the dog Boye and he became so attached to it that when he returned to England in 1642, Boye came as well to lend his support to the Royalist cause in the ensuing Civil War.

Boye became one of the few sources of inspiration and encouragement in the Royalist ranks and he soon found his way into the propaganda of the opposing forces, where he was represented as a demon and, ironically, a black dog, one of Satan's followers. When he was finally killed at the battle of Marston Moor his master wept openly.

In later life Prince Rupert was in fact accompanied by a large faithful black dog, who lived with him in retirement at Windsor. This dog filled the role of the wizard's companion and familiar spirit far better than the little white poodle, especially as his master was engaged in a variety of different scientific experiments in the Round Tower of the castle, during which he developed an improved process of mezzotint, and discovered a new formula for gunpowder.

His cousin Charles II is the only British monarch to have given his name to a breed of dog. The Merry Monarch had such an affection for toy spaniels that they lost their original name and became popularly known as King Charles spaniels. He surrounded himself with these playful little dogs, allowing them the free-run of his palace, and frequently admitting them to his bed. This intimacy did not amuse the King's subjects and not for the last time in history, voices of disapproval were raised, though tactfully out of royal earshot. Samuel Pepys commented ruefully in his diary that: 'They had access to all parts of Whitehall, even on State occasions', and he later recorded in a more critical tone: 'All I observed there was the silliness of the King playing with his dog all the while and not minding his business.'

Charles II had other favourite dogs as well, as this press notice for one which went missing indicates:

'We must call upon you again for a Black Dog between a greyhound and a spaniel, no white about him, onely a streak on his Brest, and Tayl a little bobbed. It is His Majestie's own Dog, and doubtless was stolen, for the Dog was not born nor bred in England and would never forsake his Master. Whosoever finds him may acquaint any at Whitehall, for the Dog is better known at court than those who stole him. Will they leave robbing his Majesty? Must he not keep a Dog? This Dog's place (though better than some might imagine) is the only place which nobody offers to beg.'

The early Hanoverian kings showed little interest in dogs, as in many other aspects of English life. Frederick, Prince of Wales, was presented with a puppy by Alexander Pope from his own dear dog Bounce, but even this gift from so distinguished a dog lover, and the delightful couplet which he attached to the dog's collar:

'I am His Highness' dog at Kew;
Pray, tell me, Sir, whose dog are you?'
did little to warm the Hanoverian monarchs to man's best friend.

It was left to Queen Victoria and her successors to establish the popular cult of the pet dog in all its shapes, sizes, colours and personalities. The Queen herself kept literally hundreds of dogs during her life. In the early years of her reign, her faithful companion was a spaniel named Dash, whom Lord Melbourne once inadvisably accused of having crooked legs — a comment which did little to endear him to his sovereign. But the Queen's interest was not limited solely to the occupants of the royal kennels. Throughout her life she showed a deep concern for the wellbeing of dogs everywhere, and she was one of the prime movers in curbing the appalling cruelty inflicted on animals in general.

Above right William and Richard of Gloucester favoured Australian terriers as pets – their names were Betsy and Goblin

Right In this Van Dyck portrait the children of Charles I are joined by pet spaniels. After the Restoration toy spaniels took their more familiar name from the King

Below Another royal Cairn terrier, Casper appears here with Lady Helen Windsor

Eleven years after the establishment of the Royal Society for the Prevention of Cruelty to Animals, Princess Victoria, as she then was, and her mother, the Duchess of Kent, became patrons of the society, which at the time was in a precarious financial state. This royal patronage gave a great boost to its work. Within the same year, 1835, the first bill was passed for the protection of domestic animals, and when Princess Victoria became Queen Victoria, two years later, the continued success of the Society was ensured.

Queen Victoria remained an active supporter throughout the rest of her sixty-four years on the throne. As President of the R.S.P.C.A. Lord Aberdare once described her participation in these glowing terms:

'The Society does not possess a more active member than the Queen herself . . . Many things that escape less observant eyes attract her attention and prove her to be a vigilant apostle of humanity.'

In her Diamond Jubilee year she attended the Society's annual meeting and prize-giving and put forward the idea of issuing a special medal to those who had been foremost in its work. When the design for the medal was submitted to the palace for her royal approval, Queen Victoria noticed that no cat appeared amongst the commemoration animals, and returned the draft with her own sketch of a cat that it might be included.

The waifs and strays of London's streets have reason to be grateful to the benign Queen as well. As a patron of the Lost Dogs' Home at Battersea she was successful in persuading the management committee to keep all the dogs in their care for two days longer than the period required by law, and this practice is still observed.

While his wife's affection for spaniels linked her with the Stuart monarchs, with whom she felt a close affinity, Prince Albert's were directed to the oldest, and traditionally most favoured breed, the greyhound.

His particular favourite for many years was a bitch named Eos, who, like Jowler before her, suffered at the hands of royal marksmanship. Fortunately when Eos was accidentally shot through the lung by Prince Ferdinand of Saxe-Coburg, her injury was minor in comparison with her predecessor's, and she made a rapid recovery. But a sudden relapse a year later indicates the no-nonsense concern which Queen Victoria showed for her dogs. Soon after Eos's recovery the Queen had commented how her performance in the field did not appear to have been seriously affected by the accident. But after the relapse the Queen acknowledged that the easy life of over-eating and living in the lap of luxury in London had weakened the bitch's health. *'Now she must be well starved, poor thing,'* wrote the Queen, *'and not allowed to sleep in beds, as she generally does.'*

Both the Queen and her consort were in the forefront of the breeding and showing of pedigree dogs, and they were responsible for introducing and popularising several of the successful modern breeds. Animal fashion has invariably looked to the throne for its lead, and whenever the sovereign's family has patronised any particular type of dog, it has not been long before it has risen to the higher placings in the popularity league. Welsh corgis were virtually unknown until 1933 when a newspaper photograph appeared showing Princess Elizabeth carefully leading the peculiar little dog over a railway bridge at Glamis in Scotland, yet in a comparatively short time the breed had overtaken the fox terrier in the national popularity stakes.

Above left *There is little mention of cats in the history of royal pets, but Alexandra certainly included them in her household*
Below left *Cocky, the white cockatoo often accompanied his mistress about the house*
Below *Queen Alexandra kept an enormous variety of pets. Here she sits on board the 'Osborne' with some of her dogs*

The Skye terrier had been hunting and grappling with vermin like foxes, badgers, pine martens and even wild cats for centuries before it became a pampered household pet. According to legend, the first Skyes had swum ashore from the wrecks of the Spanish Armada which had come to grief in the Hebrides. John Kayes, or Keyes, who gave his latinized name, Caius, to the college in Cambridge, and styled himself as *'a profound clerke and ravennous devourer of learning'* described in his treatise *Of English Dogges*, *'A Cur brought out the barbarous borders fro' the uttermost countryes northward which be reason of the length heare makes showe neither of face or body'*, which was most likely the Skye terrier.

Kayes was the court physician of Edward VI, Queen Mary and Queen Elizabeth I, but even these august connections made no impact in favour of the Skye among the Tudor dog-owning public. It was not until 1842 when the Victorian public saw their Queen with Rona, the best known of all Skyes, that the little dog was raised from relative obscurity to comparative popularity.

H.R.H. Princess of Wales on board the "Osborne"

Public curiosity was aroused by another highland import eighteen years later when the inhabitants of Windsor noticed some unusually shaggy denizens of the royal kennels being exercised in Windsor Great Park. These were the Queen's rough collies which, like the Skye terriers had been controlling sheep on the moors and glens of Scotland for hundreds of years before they caught the Queen's eye on her first visit to Balmoral.

The collie's rough highland background was quickly overshadowed by the new elegance it acquired. Wealthy enthusiasts on both sides of the Atlantic paid high prices for the best specimens, until eventually one was sold for one thousand pounds.

A similar stir was caused in 1860, when Looty suddenly burst upon the European canine world. A far cry from the humble breeds that had previously been elevated by royal patronage, Looty was one of the fabled and legendary lap dogs of imperial China, a Pekinese. Like many objects of curiosity from China, Looty was acquired by force. When British troops had broken into the hallowed confines of the Imperial Palace, they found the dead body of a Chinese princess who, too proud to flee, had killed herself rather than be taken captive by infidels. In her zeal to do away with herself, however, it appeared that she had overlooked the royal edict which commanded that all the royal dogs should be destroyed to prevent them from falling into alien hands. The Dragoon Guards who found her dead also found four of these dogs alive and one of them, suitably named, was presented to the Queen; another symbol of her international omnipotence.

When a few more Pekinese arrived in Britain by more orthodox means a few years later it became possible to breed from them, and since that time they have ranked among the top twenty dogs in the country.

Queen Victoria also helped to popularize the Pomeranian, though in a different form from the dog's ancestors. The original Pomeranians were large, working dogs that came from the Arctic Circle, where they were used to tend sheep and pull small carts. By the time the Queen first saw some in Florence in 1888 they had shrunk in size to between fifteen and twenty pounds, and when she bred them in England herself, the size she preferred was some four pounds smaller than that.

However, Her Majesty's predilections were soon overtaken by a popular demand for miniature specimens of the breed. It had been previously discovered that occasional small puppies were born in otherwise perfectly normal litters, and that by breeding these it was possible to produce miniatures that perfectly resembled the original full-size dog, but which weighed a mere six pounds.

Set against these tiny specimens in the show-ring, the Queen's Poms looked monstrous and they gradually fell from favour, while the others rose in popularity, until the present day champions which weigh in the region of only four pounds.

Queen Victoria first showed her Pomeranians at the first of the world-famous Dog Shows organised by Charles Cruft, at the Agricultural Hall in Islington. Her entries Fluffy, Nino, Mino, Beppo, Gilda and Lulu all won prizes that year, and though the Pomeranians gradually lost ground in their class, the Queen won many other prizes with her dogs in the last ten years of her life.

When she died at Osborne on 22 January 1901, her favourite black Pomeranian was lying peacefully at the foot of his mistress's bed, as still and quiet as the marble figure with which she had immortalized Eos at the foot of her husband's tomb in the Memorial Chapel at Windsor. Queen Victoria had always taken great care in paying her last respects to her pets; their graves at Windsor

were frequently decorated with flowers, and with her death the eighty-three dogs that survived her lost a loving and devoted mistress.

Fortunately for the royal pets, and the dog world in general, King Edward VII had inherited his mother's close attachment to her four-footed friends, and his wife, Queen Alexandra, has gone down in history as the royal pet collector par excellence.

As Prince of Wales, Edward had become the first royal patron of the Battersea Dogs' Home. He shared his wife's horror of cruelty to animals, and one of his first acts as King was to disband the pack of royal bloodhounds which had been kept for hundreds of years to hunt the tame deer at Windsor.

Edward also became the first royal patron of the Kennel Club through which he instigated an enquiry into the sickening cross-channel trade in old horses. He was also one of the most vehement opponents of the cruel practice of cropping dogs' ears, which was quickly prohibited as a result of his outspoken condemnation.

Left At stations and airports, this is a familiar sight. When the Queen travels, the dogs go with her
Below When the royal family decide to take a stroll the dogs inevitably follow. Here the whole contingent is assembled at Balmoral

After his mother's death, the new King moved all her dogs to his home at Sandringham, and closed the vast royal kennels at Windsor. There his own interests revolved around breeding gun dogs, at which he was extremely successful, leaving the proliferation of other pedigree breeds to his wife.

Throughout his life, however, the King was never without one particular pet which would accompany him everywhere. Two of these favourites were a couple of rough little terriers called Jock and Caesar.

Jock endeared himself to his royal master only a few days after his first arrival at his house. The little terrier escaped one evening and spent an enjoyable few hours roaming the streets while the house was turned upside down in the vain search to find him. Well after midnight Jock sauntered home and was immediately whisked up to his master's bedroom where he curled himself up in front of the fire and fell fast asleep. Edward was delighted when he found that he had come to no harm, and he admired the dog who, like himself, enjoyed a night out on the town. They became firm friends after that.

Jock for his part was very protective of his master. Woe betide any of the gun dogs who strayed too near the King when Jock was about: woe betide, too, the occasional hapless visitor to whom Jock took a dislike. One such victim was Joseph Chamberlain, who suffered the indignity of being pursued down the stairs at Buckingham Palace with Jock snapping at his heels.

The terrier also developed a healthy appetite for cloth, and several guests at the palace left official receptions unaware that Jock had been happily making a meal out of their tailcoats while they were otherwise engaged.

There was one memorable incident in Paris when Jock made improper advances to the pet poodle of an elderly Parisian matron in the gardens of the Tuileries. Shocked by his behaviour the old lady let fly at him with her umbrella. The King's detective, who was looking after Jock at that time, was appalled when he saw this, and rushed up to the woman protesting: 'Please! It's the King's dog!'

Left In August 1933, Princess Elizabeth was photographed with her mother and sister crossing the bridge at Glamis station – from that moment on the royal corgis were in the public eye

Opposite above In this childhood photograph the Queen Mother shows the love of animals for which she is renowned

Opposite below Another generation of royal pets! Here George V is joined by Queen Mary, Princess Mary and the dog

'So much the worse,' said the old lady as she swept off in disgust.

The little dog that mirrored his master in many ways sadly died from choking. The King was very upset by this, and he had a bracelet made from Jock's hair which he kept on his writing table for this rest of his life.

Jock's successor, Caesar, was a fox terrier who rapidly filled the void left in the King's affections. Caesar wore a collar on which was written: 'I am Caesar. I belong to the King.' Like Jock he became a close companion of his master, who insisted on feeding him himself, although he had a servant to wash him three times a week and brush him daily.

Caesar proved to be just as protective of the King as Jock had ever been. He was not unknown to chase the pets at many of the houses where he and the King were guests, and on one occasion he killed the two pet rabbits which belonged to one of the little daughters of Lord Redesdale.

He pined for days after Edward VII died. He refused to eat any of the food prepared for him by the palace staff, and spent his sad hours sitting miserably outside the door of his dead master's bedroom. It was Queen Alexandra who finally found him shivering under the King's bed, and at last persuaded him to eat something. Once she had achieved this breakthrough, Caesar came under her spell and was content to join her impressive menagerie.

Queen Alexandra was also responsible for one of the most touching sights at the King's funeral. Knowing how fond her husband had been of the little dog, she suggested that Caesar should follow the gun-carriage carrying his coffin during the funeral procession; and four years after Caesar died she added his effigy at the base of his master's tomb in St. George's Chapel, Windsor.

The Queen was herself renowned for her great love of animals. There were countless stories of her many acts of charity to waifs and strays from the whole animal kingdom. Scarcely a year after becoming Queen, she spent two hundred pounds on assorted animals at a charity fair, in one afternoon. Among her purchases she numbered Persian and

Left *Since the 1950's labradors bred at Sandringham have joined the corgis in the royal household*

Right *On his 30th birthday Prince Charles was photographed at Balmoral with Harvey, the labrador*

Siamese cats, a terrier puppy, a flying fox, two kids and a marmoset. These were duly sent along to the palace where, with the lack of suitable accommodation, they were housed in a spare room for the night, from which they escaped — causing havoc for the staff.

At Sandringham she collected an even wider assortment of animals, including monkeys, bears and even tigers, which eventually had to be sent to the London Zoo. One morning one of her large bears named Charlie escaped from his pit and wandered into a neighbouring paddock to enjoy a brief spell of freedom. Several of the estate workers spent an anxious hour in persuading him to return to his home with brooms and rakes.

Queen Alexandra is probably best remembered for her tall, stately borzoi dogs. One of her favourites, Alex, stood as high as her waist, and won more than one hundred prizes for her during his career, and in 1904 another, Sandringham Moscow, won a first for her at Crufts, while in the same competition her Samoyed Jacko, the first ever seen in Britain, came second.

In later life, Queen Alexandra spent most of her time at Sandringham, and her son George V did not take control of the kennels until after his mother's death in 1925. He then followed his father's interest in gun dogs principally, although he had five close pets throughout his life, a collie cross-bred terrier, a sealyham (which, like the present day corgis, was something of a royal trade mark), and two cairns.

In later life, King George V's Sealyham, Jack, developed the curious practice of fainting with pleasure when he saw familiar faces. On the last occasion he saw his master, in 1928, he fainted three times.

Happy, Jack's predecessor, holds the unique distinction among royal dogs of having published a book. Whether or not the text was 'ghost' written, it is Happy's name that appears on the cover, and his is the name under which the book is listed in the catalogue. The book, which is a combination of a monograph on kingship and a guide to aspiring royal pets, goes under the title of *If I Were King George.*

The Duke of Windsor followed his late father's attraction to cairns. His favourite was an attractive bitch named Cora, who used to sleep on the corner of her master's bed, and when rheumatism prevented her from jumping up, in her declining years, he had a pair of wooden steps made so that she could walk up to bed.

At the time of the Abdication crisis his constant companion was another cairn called Slipper, whose well-being was so important to the King that before going into exile he managed to find time to arrange with London's leading canine beauty parlour for half a dozen special trimming combs, instructions as to how to use them and any other articles of a dog's boudoir that he might need, to be sent to him before he and Slipper left for France, after the Abdication broadcast had been made.

Following his marriage to Mrs. Simpson, he gradually became attached to her favourite breed, the pug, which had first been introduced into England by William of Orange. They bred pugs at their home in France with as much enthusiasm as the royal family were breeding labradors and corgis in England, and in 1956 two of their pugs, Trooper and Davy Crockett, won first and second prizes respectively at the International Dog Show in Paris.

The story of our own Queen's love of dogs really starts with the gift of a cairn puppy from her uncle, the Prince of Wales, presented to her on her third birthday. Both Princess Elizabeth's parents were fond of dogs. Her mother had been given a Sealyham, Billy, as a wedding present, and her father, the Duke of York, was a keen shot and therefore shared his father's interest in sporting dogs.

The Duke of York's family started life at 145 Piccadilly, in the heart of London. Princess Elizabeth and Princess Margaret Rose often went to play with the children of Viscount Weymouth, in their garden which was next to Hyde Park, and frequently their games were joined by the Weymouths' pet corgi. Inevitably the two little girls began to ask their parents if they could have a dog like their friends' and, pleased that their children showed signs of being as dog-minded as they were, their parents enquired from the Weymouths' breeder if there were any more to be bought.

Mr. Gray, the breeder's husband, brought three corgi puppies to 145 Piccadilly for the family to inspect. Two were tailless but the other had a short, stumpy tail which was the deciding factor in the Duchess's opinion. The dog must have something to wag, she told her children, otherwise how were they to know that it was happy. The chosen puppy was sent back to Mrs. Gray's kennels to be house-trained and unofficially to be given the name which has gone down in history as that of the first royal corgi — Dookie.

Whereas many of Queen Victoria's dogs had originated in Scotland, Dookie and his successors were the descendants of the cattle dogs of Wales, where corgis had a reputation of being fiercely loyal to their owners and equally aggressive to anyone else — a reputation which many associated with Buckingham Palace will certainly confirm.

After the family moved to Royal Lodge, Windsor, they had the chance to expand their family of pets. By this time Dookie had been joined by a corgi bitch, Lady Jane, though their relationship was never more than a platonic one and in order to further the cause of royal corgis Jane had to seek a husband elsewhere. Her searches were successful and Christmas 1938 was made all the more festive by the birth of Crackers and Carol on Christmas Eve.

Among the other dogs that the family gathered around them were Choo-Choo, a Tibetan lion dog, which the King referred to as 'an animated dish cloth' and 'hairy monster', a black cocker spaniel called Ben, and a

Left *The beloved corgi lends charm to this formal portrait taken in 1938*

Right *Prince Andrew sits with some more royal spaniels in the Balmoral kennels*

golden retriever called Judy.

Until her death in 1944 Jane was always looked upon as Princess Elizabeth's dog, and when she was run over in Windsor Great Park by one of the estate staff, it was Princess Elizabeth who wrote to the driver to tell him that she was sure that it was not his fault. Jane, she knew, had a habit of getting excited and dashing in front of cars.

Throughout the early years of the war, the two Princesses were kept very much out of the public eye, and the rumour that they had been evacuated to Canada was deliberately never denied. During this time the companionship of their pets must have been a very important part of their lives and the ability of being taken out of herself which the Queen appears to find in tending to her pets today, may well stem from these years of comparative isolation during the war.

By the time Princess Elizabeth married Lieutenant Philip Mountbatten, something of a tradition had been established of royal dogs accompanying their owners on their honeymoons. Slipper had gone into exile with the Duke of Windsor, and the Duke of Kent and Princess Marina had been attended on their honeymoon by the Duke's favourite Alsatian, Lion. So it was not such a great surprise that, when the young couple left Buckingham Palace to drive to the station at the start of their honeymoon, they were accompanied by the Princess's corgi, Susan.

Susan in her turn gave birth to more puppies, one of whom, Sugar, was the mother of Whisky and Sherry which were given to Prince Charles and Princess Anne at Christmas, 1955.

In spite of the royal family's strong affection for corgis, the little dogs have followed their predecessors at times in their penchant for attacking innocent passers-by.

Susan bit a guardsman at Buckingham Palace in 1954. Four months later Honey took a bite out of a policeman. And in August 1956 when Prince Charles, his sister and their nanny were taking her for a walk in St. James's Park, Honey suddenly took off across the grass and launched herself at the seat of an off-duty Guards officer, tearing the back of his trousers in a very alarming way. Prince Charles was very concerned, but the officer had time to assure him that he was quite all right, before he hurried away to change into something less compromising.

1962 saw the birth of Heather who for fifteen years was the matriarch of the royal corgis and the ancestor of Foxy, Tiny and Busy, and the next generation which included Brush, the mother of Prince Andrew's and Prince Edward's earliest pets, Jolly and Fox.

The royal children have all been brought up to feed and groom their pets themselves and the Queen also finds time to feed her own corgis, mixing meat, gravy and dog biscuits in the way that each of them likes, just as Queen Victoria did a hundred years ago.

Since the 1950's labradors bred at Sandringham have become important adjuncts to the royal menagerie, primarily as working gun dogs, but also as amiable country companions. Prince Charles has frequently been seen with a pet labrador. In 1959 he posed with a favourite called Flame, and in both the official photographs which he chose to mark his twenty-fourth and his thirtieth birthdays he is seen with other labrador friends.

Labradors are popular with other members of the royal family too. Princess Alexandra's children James and Marina both owned one, while their mother became well known for her pet Chow called Muff.

Princess Margaret looked as if she would follow her grandfather's taste for Sealyhams when she acquired Johnny. However, during a period of quarantine which followed immediately after his arrival, and prevented him from seeing his mistress, the Sealyham transferred his affections to the Queen Mother who had been looking after him — and that was that.

Left *Prince Charles and the Queen Mother share the company of Pippin. Windsor, 1954*
Above right *The Queen and Sugar photographed at Balmoral in 1952*

However, in the 1960's Princess Margaret and the Earl of Snowdon acquired a Cavalier King Charles spaniel, a sort of transatlantic cousin of the Stuart favourites, which they called Rowley, an amusing reference to Charles II whose nickname had been Old Rowley.

Dogs have become so much part and parcel of the British monarchy that it is easy to forget that there have ever been any other royal pets, but birds, rabbits and even a lamb have all received their share of royal affection.

Katharine of Aragon brought her pet parrot to England with her when she came to marry Prince Arthur, and it was still alive when she married his brother Henry VIII. But birds really became popular as pets after the Restoration. Charles II was particularly fond of them and he created the lake in St. James's Park which became a haven for all types of birds. Birdcage Walk along the southern side of the park takes its name from the wicker

baskets in which the Keeper of the King's Birds housed his master's favourites. With the exception of the hereditary Grand Falconer, the Duke of St. Albans, only members of the royal family were permitted to use the carriage way along the Walk until it was opened to the public in 1828.

John Evelyn mentions in his diary a crane in the King's lake, which, after an unfortunate accident, had been fitted with an artificial leg. Another amusing anecdote shows some insight into Charles II's sense of humour. Feeding his ducks, hat in hand, one afternoon, the King was approached by the Lord Mayor of London who had come to see him on a matter of some urgency. Before proceeding with his business the Mayor suggested that it might be proper for the King to replace his hat but His Majesty waved this aside saying wryly: 'No matter, my Lord Mayor. It is to the ducks that I take off my hat.'

Frances Stuart, Duchess of Lennox and Richmond, who was known for her beauty as 'La Belle', was always a great favourite of King Charles's. Whether or not she was equally attached to the king, she doted on her pet African grey parrot for over forty years. When she died, however, the bird is believed to have survived her for only a few days, before giving up the ghost itself. Her executors, knowing her attachment to the bird, had it stuffed and placed beside her tomb, where it can still be seen in the Undercroft of Westminster Abbey.

The vogue for exotic birds lasted right through the eighteenth century and reached its peak during the Regency when parrots, macaws, canaries, parakeets and wax-bills became the *sine qua non* of high society. Queen Victoria's mother was always surrounded by her pet birds and the Princess, her daughter, inherited this love of birds. Among the graves of her pets at Windsor there is a small headstone in memory of her favourite bullfinch, Bully.

Queen Victoria's senior daughter-in-law,

Princess Alexandra, arrived in England for her wedding to the Prince of Wales with two turtle doves which she had owned since her childhood — a move guaranteed to win the hearts of her new subjects. From that day on the beautiful Danish Princess was marked down as an animal lover. On her first visit to Ireland she stepped ashore and was immediately presented with a white dove, the emblem of peace. This became Willie, who joined the now growing royal aviary, and from whom all the Irish doves at Sandringham are descended.

Queen Alexandra bred and showed prize-winning bantams at Sandringham too, but her favourite bird was probably her white cockatoo with a perfect salmon pink crest, called Cocky. The bird used to call his mistress Alexandra and used to accompany her throughout the house. Cocky suffered a brain storm, however. He systematically stripped himself of all his magnificent white feathers and had to be banished to another room in the end, when he started to whistle and scream like a steam engine.

Far left *The Duke and Duchess of Windsor arrive at the Gare St. Lazare, with their four pugs. Paris, 1960*

Left *Rowley, the King Charles spaniel, accompanies Princess Margaret as she leaves for Balmoral. On this occasion three corgi puppies also travelled on the train – in crates*

Right *Another departure scene. The Queen seems hardly to know which way to turn*

King George V was seldom without his grey-pink parrot, Charlotte. At Sandringham she would come into breakfast perched lightly on the King's finger and during the meal she would spend her time nonchalantly wandering over the table carefully examining the butter, jam, sugar, or whatever tasty dish took her fancy.

George V was also fond of budgerigars. He had an aviary built off his dressing-room so that he could potter along the cages talking to the birds and feeding them through the bars. His granddaughter, Princess Elizabeth, followed his example when she was nine. Among her impressive menagerie of pets which include corgis, collies, two fawns and some ponies, there were fifteen blue budgerigars, which over the years have risen to a present-day total of nearer fifty.

The nursery at Buckingham Palace has been filled with the sounds of other animals apart from the yap of corgis. Prince Charles owned a rabbit named Harvey, a hamster named Chi-Chi and two South African love birds, which he called David and Annie, after

David Crockett and Annie Oakley.

His great-aunt, Princess Mary, had become something of an expert on rabbits during her youth. In 1919 she won two first prizes and a second for her rabbits at the King's Lynn Fur and Feather Show. The following year she again won, this time collecting two firsts, two seconds and a third, and her silver, fawn and blue Beveran rabbits continued this winning run for many years.

All the signs suggest that the Queen's first grandchild, Peter Phillips, will inherit the royal family's fondness for animals. With his parents as two leading world-class riders, a country upbringing surrounded by animals, and a family devoted to virtually everything that walks on four legs or flies in the air, he will be the first in the next generation of royal pet owners to continue this historic tradition.

Even if the Queen was prevented from following her own ideal of spending a life in the country surrounded by lots of horses and dogs, she has made certain that her daughter and her family will have the opportunities denied her.

ROYAL SPORTING ANIMALS

*R*acing may be the Sport of Kings but without doubt the most ancient of royal pursuits is hunting. An old Welsh proverb: *'You may know a gentleman by his horse, his hawk and his greyhound'* indicates that the nobility was well-versed in the art of the chase.

Greyhounds were highly prized by many British monarchs, both as hunting animals, as well as pets, though no doubt many of their subjects took a different view of this royal obsession. The Bishop of Winchester must have been less than amused when King John occasionally descended on him at Farnham Castle, accompanied by his pack of two hundred and forty greyhounds, to stay for a week at a time.

The treatment and attention given to hunting hounds must have raised a few eyebrows among the peasantry as well, whose own treatment at royal hands was often far less considerate. Hounds often wore collars made of coloured leather, or even silk, decorated with silver or gold lettering and often hung with bells.

An early fifteenth century manual on hunting, *Livre de Chasse*, gives clear instructions on the care that should be taken with hunting dogs. The hounds, it states, should always be attended by a boy, whose responsibility it was to groom them and keep them happy. This boy should exercise the hounds and should *'...lead them in some fair place where tender grass groweth ... for to take their medicine. For sometimes hounds seek with grass, that he eateth ... and healeth himself.'*

The Queen takes an interest in the Beaufort hounds. Badminton, 1978

Great attention was paid too to the correct breeding of these highly prized animals. Writing in 1408 one Juliana Berners stated:
'A greyhound should be headed lyke a snake
And neckyd lyke a drake
Footed lyke a cat
Tayled lyke a rat
Syded lyke a teem
Chymed lyke a beme'.
Modern breeding standards may be more accurate, but they lack such visual impact.

The illustrious white hunting dogs of the French monarchy were probably the ancestors of most of the hounds in Europe today. They almost certainly gave rise to the medieval Talbot, a white hound-like dog, with floppy ears and prodigious powers of scent.

Talbots, or hounds very like them, were used to hunt deer in sixteenth century England, while greyhounds were usually reserved for coursing hares, and spaniels for falconry and fowling. A gift of a pair of greyhounds was a sure way of gaining favour with King Henry VIII, and James I was so attached to his hunting dogs that he knew the names of all his hounds and beagles by heart.

Prince Rupert, who in adult life showed such affection for his poodle Boye, nearly lost his life while trying to save a favourite hound when he was still a boy. Noticing the dog disappear down a hole in hot pursuit of a fox, and then fail to reappear, the intrepid Prince squeezed inside the hole himself to rescue it. He managed to grab hold of one of its legs and then found that he was stuck himself.

Fortunately, a fellow huntsman saw his feet sticking out of the hole and deftly pulled him out together with the dog, still holding onto the fox.

It was during the reign of the Stuart kings that the packs of royal hounds became firmly established and many of them were still in existence at the beginning of this century. George IV hunted a pack of dwarf beagles and the royal bloodhounds were pursuing deer right up until they were disbanded by Edward VII.

In the twentieth century, however, the royal interest in sporting dogs has been concentrated almost exclusively on the breeding and training of gun dogs; most of which has taken place at Sandringham.

King Edward VII introduced clumber spaniels to the Sandringham kennels because, as he maintained: 'A clumber can do the work of three beaters'.

Although classified as a spaniel, the clumber is quite unlike any other variety. It is a large, long-bodied dog, with a square head and heavy, beetling brows, that together give the impression that it was formed from the cross between a St. Bernard and a golden retriever. Sturdy, strong and rather ponder-

ous in their gait, clumbers are very useful when working in thick undergrowth and were greatly favoured by sportsmen at the turn of the century, although they have fallen in popularity since then. One Edwardian enthusiast wrote: '*He (the Clumber) is one of the most useful and popular of the several varieties of Sporting Spaniels. He is also one of the oldest. He is at once the most dignified and yet most docile. Most daring and yet most tractable.*' In fact the clumber was ideally suited both in temperament and pace to the requirements of the aging King.

George V assumed control of the Sandringham kennels after his mother's death and, from then on, he devoted them to gun dogs. King George greatly favoured his father's heavy clumbers, although he also introduced black labradors of his own.

The King insisted that only dogs capable of working four or five days a week should be allowed to occupy one of his kennels and, under this rigid policy, the kennels at Wolferton and at Sandringham produced a succession of outstanding gun dogs during the mid-war years.

Wolferton Shelah developed the rare ability of running along the line of beaters whenever summoned by the Head Keeper's horn. The dog would run from one beater to the next until coming to the Head Keeper, but even over distances of up to two miles, she would never take a short cut across a line.

Between 1871 and 1935 there were only two Head Keepers at Sandringham, and the continued success of the royal dogs owed a lot to the dedication, loyalty and consistency that was shown by them.

In 1935 the best gun dog at Sandringham was Sandringham Stow, who had previously won two first prizes and three seconds at shows in 1932, and in 1934 and 1935 was first at the King's Lynn Show.

Sandringham Spark was perhaps the best of the King's clumbers, and he was succeeded by Sandringham Scion, which co-incidentally died within a few hours of his master.

Sandringham Scrum and Sandringham Bob were two of the King's favourite labradors, Bob being a popular name of the King's,

Left Young Prince Charles confronts a disobedient foxhound. He has the Hunt Master's authority but seems unsure about his next move – especially as the miscreant is so friendly

Below Queen Alexandra's famous borzois were for show and not for hunting

and one which he later gave to his pet cairn.

Labradors were favourites with George VI, too. At Royal Lodge, Windsor, he kept three, Mimsy, Stiffy and Scrummy, and in 1948 another, Windsor Bob, came first in the Kennel Club's retriever trials. This is the biggest test of the year for any gun dog, and in 1948 it quickly turned into a duel between the King's yellow labrador and a black labrador, Scotney Kinsman, owned by the film magnate Joseph Arthur Rank. For two days the dogs ran and swam after downed bird and runners, while the judges assessed their performance under a variety of conditions. Windsor Bob brought every bird back without making a mistake, but Scotney Kinsman missed a runner at the end of the first day, which cost him the coveted first place. The King was delighted with the success of the dog he had used many times while shooting at Sandringham, and for whom he held great respect.

Quiet and undemonstrative as he was, King George VI cared deeply for his dogs and one of the last things he did on the eve of his death was to twice visit one of his faithful pack which had injured its paw during the day's shooting.

The tradition of breeding top-class labradors has continued at Sandringham under the present Queen. They are used frequently by Prince Charles and Prince Philip whenever they are shooting on the estate, and one was presented to the French President, Monsieur Giscard d'Estaing, when he paid a state visit to Britain a few years ago.

In recent years royal shooting has itself come under fire from anti-bloodsports protestors. Shortly after the publication of his book *The Environmental Revolution,* Prince Philip defended the royal family's hunting and shooting pursuits as being no more immoral than factory farming.

Prince Charles was labelled 'hooligan of the year' by one incensed official of the R.S.P.C.A. following a visit to Austria, during which he shot wild boar and pheasant. 'The fact that I go shooting is not because I enjoy massacring other creatures,' the Prince explained in his defence. 'I really do enjoy ani-

mals and I deeply revel in nature. . . If people didn't partake in country sports there would not be many animals and there would not be the countryside we have now.'

However, the average bag at a royal shoot nowadays is considerably smaller than the slaughter of thousands of birds that took place when George V was alive, and the practice of big game hunting in Africa and tiger hunting in India has died out completely. The last royal tiger fell to Prince Philip in 1961 and since then he has espoused the cause of wildlife protection, while maintaining his own firm belief in the validity of shooting game birds. 'There is a vast difference between an intelligent cropping of an abundant stock and the threat to a diminishing number in one species', he explained to one television interviewer. And on another occasion he answered critics with the reasoned argument that modern technology, and the ecological and environmental changes which it has brought about, has caused the extinction of many animal species. 'What man the hunter has failed to do in millions of years,' he concluded, 'man as a businessman and scientist is achieving in a couple of generations, and with general approval.'

Before the shotgun was adopted as a sporting fire-arm, the most common way of hunting birds on the wing was the art of falconry, and the possession of a cast of falcons was as much a status symbol in those days as a pack of fine hounds.

Medieval kings went to great lengths to procure their birds of prey. Every year Henry II sent to Pembrokeshire for the young falcons that were to be found in the coastal cliffs. His son King John obtained his from as far afield as Ireland.

Falcons accompanied kings on all their travels. King Harold seldom appears in the Bayeux Tapestry without a well-developed bird perched on his wrist, and some one hundred and twenty years after Harold's defeat at Hastings Richard the Lionheart's falcons were swooping on their prey above the barren plains of the Middle East.

Edward III, with whom the heraldic falcon is most closely associated, delighted in the

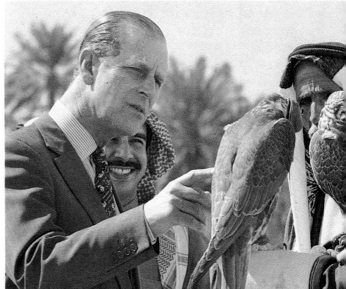

SVI MILITES:EQVI TANT: AD BOS HAC

Above *King Harold rides with his hounds by his side and a hawk on his arm – a scene from the Bayeux tapestry*

Below left *Prince Philip inspects a falcon on his recent visit to Bahrain*

sport. When he was fifteen years old he received a falcon as a peace offering from the King of Scotland, for which he paid the falconer forty shillings. Philippa, his wife and Queen, brought her falconers with her when she came to England from Flanders. And when Edward and his son the Black Prince invaded France, they took thirty falconers with them to provide sport between their battles.

The laws protecting falcons were ruthless in their penalties. In 1363, Edward III proclaimed: 'If any man steal a hawk and the same carry away, it shall be done of him as of a thief of a horse,' and the penalty for stealing a horse was death. Henry VII imposed a penalty of imprisonment for a year and a day on anyone convicted of stealing falcons' eggs, which greatly helped to protect the native supply of birds.

Until 1537 the royal falcons were housed in the mews on the site of what is today the National Gallery. The word 'mews' was derived from an Old French word meaning a change, particularly of coat or feathers, and the mews was where the king's falcons were kept during their moulting period.

Henry VIII symbolised the Tudor ideal of the Renaissance sovereign. His passion for hunting and hawking was known throughout Europe and the gift of a cast of hawks to the King of England was guaranteed to meet with royal approval. A servant of the Duke of Ferrara who presented Henry with such a gift was handsomely reimbursed to the tune of twenty-three pounds, six shillings and eightpence. While nearer home, Anne Boleyn's personal badge, the white falcon, can only have added to her attractions in the King's eyes.

Both Elizabeth I and Mary Queen of Scots relished the sport, which reached its zenith during their lives. In Scotland Mary used to ride with her falcons accompanied by an unnerving and unlikely companion, the Presbyterian reformer John Knox. As a captive in England she was accompanied on her rides by her custodian, the Royal Falconer of England. This did not please Queen Elizabeth, and she quickly put an end to the excursions.

King James I was as keen a falconer as his mother. He wrote a treatise on hawking. He outlawed the use of fire-arms and bows for hunting game, and he banned what he referred to as 'disorderly hawking'. Charles I found the sport a relaxing diversion from the not insignificant worries of his reign, but with his fall and the chaos of the Civil War the heyday of falconry passed for ever. Charles II attempted to revive it after the Restoration, spending many happy days on the uplands around Winchester, but as one writer commented two years after the King's return: '...hawking falls not within the compass of everyone's ability to pursue, being as it were, only entailed on great persons and vast estates', and these had greatly suffered during the time of the Commonwealth.

In spite of Charles's reconstruction of the Royal Mews and the re-bestowal of the office of Hereditary Falconer of England on his elder son by Nell Gwynn, he could not stem the decline of the sport. It had virtually died out in England by the end of the eighteenth century, but survived rather longer in Scotland and in France, where the post of Grand Falconer was maintained until the French Revolution.

Falconry today is a specialist sport practised by only a few enthusiasts. However, they number among them Prince Philip, whose interest in ornithology naturally drew him to it. During a recent state visit to Bahrain he was shown round a lavish falcon breeding centre, where the birds are bred in captivity, in what looks like a comfortable modern hotel. And he has always taken an interest in the falconry displays at British shows like the Game Fair. But as far as modern sporting birds are concerned, the royal falcons have been replaced by what were once their quarry, pigeons.

The Duke of York established a loft of racing pigeons at Sandringham in 1893 and the royal pigeon lofts remained there until after his death, when they were finally removed to Gaywood, King's Lynn. Apart from competing in homing competitions, the pigeons saw active service with the RAF during the Second World War. In 1940 one of the King's pigeons brought back a message from an aircraft which had made a forced landing. For this it was awarded the Dickin medal for gallantry. The Queen follows her father's interests in racing pigeons, and characteristically has made herself as knowledgeable about the birds as the most ardent pigeon fanciers.

The Queen, however, is probably best known for her knowledge of horses and for the obvious pleasure she has derived from them throughout her life. She has her favourites, like Benbow, just as Richard II had his, Roan Barbary, and George III had Adonis.

The interest in riding horses for pleasure, as opposed to using them to fulfil a purely functional role, really developed during the reign of the first Queen Elizabeth. 'Many horses are requisite for a king', wrote ill-fated Bishop Latimer, but that maxim is equally applicable to both Elizabeths.

Henry VIII's daughter bred many different types of horse at her royal mews for the use of her court. There were 'Barbaries' which were popular as travelling horses on account of their easy pace, which was something between an amble and a trot. There were Spanish Jennets, which as mares were highly prized for breeding the most popular of all medieval

Edward stands over a wild Chillingham bull shot during a visit to the Northumberland estate

Above left *Edward VII examines the bag. Such enormous shoots were quite common in his day*

Above right *The last royal tiger fell to Prince Philip in 1961. Here George V hunts in India during his 1911-1912 tour*

riding horses, palfreys.

Queen Elizabeth I rode side-saddle as every lady had done since the time of Anne of Bohemia, the Queen of Richard II, who developed the technique. Whether hunting with hounds or falcons, or travelling through her kingdom in one of her stately progresses, Queen Bess was invariably seated on a favourite palfrey. Her followers would be mounted on a variety of different horses. The huntsmen would ride the amblers and coursers to be used by the nobles of the court when hunting. The pages and attendants would ride cobs and rouncies, while the troops that accompanied every progress were provided for by large Tudor warhorses.

King James I set even greater store by horsemanship than had his predecessor on the throne. *'But the honourablest and most commendable Games that a king can use are on Horseback,'* he wrote in his famous treatise on kingship, *Religio Regis,* or the *Faith and Duty of a Prince, 'for it becomes a Prince above all Men to be a good Horseman: And use such games on Horseback as may teach you to handle your Arms thereon; such as The Tilt, Ring and low-riding for handling your sword. As for hunting, the most honourable, and noblest sport thereof is with running Hounds; for it is a Thievish sport of hunting to shoot with guns and bow.'*

Though phrased in different terms the advice given by King George V to his eldest son shows that he attached the same significance to horsemanship as had King James. 'The English people like riding,' he told the Prince of Wales, 'and it would make you very unpopular if you could not do so. If you can't ride, you know, I am afraid the people will call you a duffer.'

James I's eldest son, Prince Charles heeded his father's advice too. An elegant horseman himself, he took care to ensure that his sons were well drilled in the kingly art. By the time Prince Charles (later Charles II) was ten he could ride and jump even the most difficult horses in the royal stable, with or without a saddle, a skill acquired thanks largely to his horse-loving tutor, the Earl of Newcastle. It was a skill on which his safety depended during the dangerous days spent as a fugitive from Cromwell's troops, after the defeat at Worcester. It was a skill which he also employed to full advantage when he returned to his kingdom in 1660, proudly riding from Dover to London accompanied by 'above twenty thousand horse and foot.'

'Our gracious and most excellent King is not only the handsomest and most comely horseman in the world,' wrote the jubilant Earl of Newcastle after his pupil's Restoration, *'but as knowing and understanding in the art as any man; and no man makes a horse go better than I have seen some go under His Majesty the first time that ever he came upon their backs, which is the height and quintessence of the art.'*

Like his modern namesake, Charles II did

not confine his riding to formal public displays and private entertainment, he frequently took part in races at his favourite Newmarket, and almost as frequently, he won. He enjoyed the easy atmosphere of the races, where he could mix with the jockeys and stable lads with an easy conviviality reminiscent of our own Queen. Not content to be a spectator, however, Charles became the only British monarch since Richard II to ride his horses first past the winning post. In 1666 he introduced the Town Plate to be raced for at Newmarket and later won it himself. The race has in fact been run at Newmarket on the second Thursday in October ever since, except for the years of the Second World War.

The cause of royal riding did not receive any great advancement from the next two British kings. However, James I was one of the first and most dedicated fox-hunters and owned the first pack of foxhounds ever kept in Britain. Until then the chase had been concerned almost exclusively with a nobler prey, the deer.

William III enjoyed hunting in Windsor Forest and was evidently delighted with the gift of one hundred and eight red deer sent from Germany to improve his sport. However, his best remembered feat of horsemanship is probably his death. His horse stumbled on a molehill when coming from Hampton Court. Thrown from his saddle, he sustained injuries from which he died. The supporters of the exiled James II raised their glasses to the 'little gentleman in black velvet' which had literally brought about the 'usurper's downfall'.

Queen Anne was dubbed 'the mightiest huntress of her age', a title which befitted the great lady, who even in later life thought nothing of pursuing a deer for forty miles or more through Windsor Forest.

She established Ascot as both the centre for her racing interest and the headquarters for her hunting. During her reign the pack of royal hounds was kennelled on the heath, and there remained until it was disbanded by Edward VII at the turn of this century.

Although she had been a keen horsewoman in her early life, the ravages of ill health, persistent child-bearing and excessive weight finally forced her to give up hunting from the saddle, and from then on she was restricted to following the chase in small chaise, or gig.

No such commendable enthusiasm for field sports was shown by either of the first two Hanoverian monarchs, who found horses and riding as little to their taste as almost every other aspect of traditional English life.

George III, however, showed himself to be as keen a hunter as his Stuart predecessors. Deer hunting was his chief interest and throughout his hunting life he was an intrepid follower of the royal buckhounds. The deer he hun-

Left *Charles I ensured that his sons also became good horsemen. This famous portrait is by Van Dyck*

Right *Princess Anne met her husband through their mutual interest in horses. Here Mark Phillips rides Great Ovation, winner of the Badminton Horse Trials, 1971*

ted were tame stags and hinds brought by cart from the five well-stocked deer paddocks at Swinley. These animals were never killed in the chase and would often provide sport for several seasons. Unlike the deer hunted by earlier kings they were pursued purely to provide entertainment, there was no longer a pressing need to provide venison for the king's banqueting table.

Queen Victoria's love of horses started when she was thirteen on the back of her favourite pony, Rosa. When she was a couple of years older, she won a chestnut mare from her uncle, William IV, and throughout her life she showed a constant attachment to horses as they enjoyed their final period of dominance before being superseded by the internal combustion engine.

As a young queen she was a very elegant figure on horseback, either when reviewing her troops from a sturdy charger or when cantering in the royal parks on Tartar, her sprightly little dark brown horse, discussing the current affairs of state with the Prime Minister, Lord Melbourne.

The Prince Consort was idolized by his wife, and few pleasures were greater for her than to ride beside him at Windsor or at Osborne, mounted on the chestnut Hammon, which had been presented to her by the King of Prussia in 1844.

Balmoral also provided many opportunities for them to ride together. The stocky highland ponies served equally well to transport the Queen and her sketching materials as they did to act as stalking ponies, carrying Prince Albert's bag down from the moors after a successful day's stag shooting. And it was only the arrival of John Brown and the Queen's favourite highland pony at Osborne, which finally restored her spirits after the Prince Consort's death. Even in her widow's weeds the Queen was able to enjoy excursions on Fyvie, led by her faithful 'highland servant' and when in later life she could no longer ride, like Queen Anne, she took to driving herself about the parks and gardens of her various homes in small donkey carts, or little carriages drawn by docile ponies.

Both Edward VII and Queen Alexandra were regular hunters throughout their married life, although as Princess of Wales, Alexandra's participation met with strong disapproval from her mother-in-law, who took many years to become reconciled to the habit of Victorian women riding to hounds.

However, the Queen was an enthusiastic supporter of fox hunting for men since it was looked upon as an increasingly democratic sport, an aspect which strongly appealed to her egalitarian sentiments.

With the passing of Edward VII royal riding took on more of the qualities of the country squire and lost many of its more formal and ceremonial trappings. King George V advised his sons to ride, on the basis that the people expected it of them, and he always attended military parades and reviews on horseback. However, the formal rides of Queen Victoria and her courtiers through the royal parks in London had passed for ever. The King and his family might be seen riding in London, but this was very much a recreational pastime and was conducted on the same principle as their private riding at Balmoral, Windsor or Sandringham.

George V used to ride from beat to beat during the shoots on his various estates and in the course of this he formed a lifelong attachment to a white cob called Jock. Jock was used at Sandringham and Balmoral for shooting and for quiet potters about the estates, visiting tenants and looking round the farms.

While his father enjoyed the sedate company of Jock, the Prince of Wales sought more stimulating equine company. He started to hunt while at university and quickly discovered the thrill of steeplechasing which matched his taste for adventure. Although Prince Edward was technically less proficient than his brother Bertie, his daring riding and carefree abandon in the hunting field made him a popular figure throughout the riding world. On his tours of the Empire he experienced forms of riding as different as herding cattle in Canada and pig sticking in India.

He learned to play polo, as his father had done, and he took part in point-to-points, becoming the first heir apparent for four hundred years to ride in a race and win it. In 1921 he won his first race under national hunt rules and was presented with the winning trophy by his proud parents. But, as with his desire to serve in the army during the Great War, these attempts to prove his worth in open competition with others were stymied by his parents. In 1924 he fell at the first fence in the army point-to-point at Arborfield Cross and concussed himself so badly that he had to stay in bed for a month. There had been frequent reports in the press on both sides of

the Atlantic about his racing accidents and this latest one prompted a public outcry against the risks that he appeared to be taking. His father and the Prime Minister both pleaded with him to desist from this unnecessarily dangerous sport, but it was another four years before he finally agreed to hang up his riding boots and sell his hunters.

In the meantime the quieter and more evidently conscientious Duke of York was proving himself to be the best horseman in the

family. He was as fond of hunting as his older brother though far less reckless, and it was only in accordance with strict royal economy during the Depression that he reluctantly gave up the sport. Throughout his life, though, he took great pleasure in riding whenever time allowed. Before breakfast was always a popular time of the day with him, and as soon as his two daughters were old enough to ride he used to accompany them on their ponies in Windsor Park.

Princess Elizabeth had her first riding lesson when she was two and a half, and she was given her first pony for Christmas a year later, in 1929. Ponies and dogs were to play an important part in the 'normal' upbringing which the Duke and Duchess of York envisaged for their daughters. Peggy, as this first pony was called, was followed by others as the two Princesses became increasingly 'pony minded'. George was presented to them straight from the pit-head of a Durham coal mine; Gem was iron-mouthed and thick-necked, and therefore difficult for little girls to handle; and Snowball came from the shafts of a jaunting-car in Ireland and had the annoying habit of walking round in circles when required to go forwards. But as well as these there were more successful mounts on which the young Princesses were able to develop their riding skills under the watchful eye of Owen, one of the royal grooms.

Greylight and Comet were two of the longest serving pre-war ponies on which the royal children were taught to walk, trot and canter without stirrups, in the Royal Riding School at Buckingham Palace. But with the outbreak of war, these lessons stopped and the two Princesses found themselves riding in a totally new environment, at Balmoral.

Here they schooled and looked after their ponies Jock and Hans themselves, the stable staff having been reduced as a result of the war. In those early war years in Scotland the two girls were responsible for grooming the bronze-coloured Jock and dun-coloured Hans themselves. They had to feed them and muck them out as well. But these chores had their compensations. For the first time the two girls were free to ride whenever they liked, and

Above, *George V would ride his favourite cob, Jock, from beat to beat during a shoot*
Above left *Queen Victoria rides her highland pony, John Brown is in attendance. Balmoral, 1868*
Below left *Princess Anne and Prince Charles both learnt to ride this blue roan pony, William*

within reason wherever they liked, and for the only time in their lives they experienced the freedom with their ponies which other children take for granted.

With the shortage of transport Jock and Hans were broken to harness and the Princesses were taught to drive them, and the Fell ponies on the estate.

In the closing years of the war they returned to live in Windsor and the things they had learned with the ponies at Balmoral were put into practice once more. In the 1943 Royal Windsor Horse Show the seventeen-year-old Princess Elizabeth drove both the Fell pony Gypsy, and a Utility vehicle into first place. The following year she drove her sister's pony Hans to win a Driving Class.

After the war Elizabeth graduated to the horses of the Royal Mews. In public she began to deputize on horseback for her ailing father while in private she and Prince Philip began to acquire horses of their own.

Pegasus was presented to the Princess in 1951 after a career in which he had won In-Hand and Riding Classes. He remained a favourite with both the royal couple until returning to his former owner after his legs were fired five years later.

While on a visit Malta in 1954 the Queen's uncle, Lord Louis Mountbatten presented her with a grey gelding North African Barb

called Surprise. The Queen rode him for ten years and in all that time he never failed to live up to his name. Constantly playing tricks on his rider the horse was always 'a diabolical ride', in the Queen's own words, but she enjoyed mastering his antics more than any other horse she had ridden.

Over the years the Royal Mews at Windsor has housed a wide variety of horses from polo ponies to retired race horses, all of which have been ridden by the Queen and other members of the royal family at some time or another.

Betsy, the Queen's beloved black mare, bought from a local farmer in 1953, was 'top of the stables' for years. More recently Burmese and Centennial, both presented to her by the Royal Canadian Mounted Police have been housed at Windsor, performing the dual purpose of royal chargers and favourite hacks.

There have been several horses given as presents by other heads of states, which have broadened the range of breeds and temperaments. Pride, presented to the Queen by King Hussein of Jordan in 1958, became a popular mount of Princess Anne's in spite of his peculiar habit of hanging out his tongue, and won the second prize as the Best Turned Out Horse for her at Ascot in 1963.

In 1957 Mr. Kruschev and Marshal Bulganin paid a state visit to Britain and brought with them a Russian Akhal-teke stallion called Mele-Kush which they gave to Prince Philip. The horse presented quite a problem to the Ministry of Agriculture, who had never seen one quite the same colour as Mele-Kush before. After a good deal of ministerial debate, it was decided to record Mele-Kush as coloured 'Old Gold' and thanks to him a new colour was added to the official list.

Today the Queen's riding follows a regular pattern. Some of her horses are taken to Balmoral or Sandringham for her holidays there, where she and other members of the family

Left *Princess Anne takes a jump at the Montreal Olympics. She is riding her most famous horse, Goodwill*

Above *At Amberley Horse Trials, 1973, she appeared on another mount, Flame Gun*

Below *Here she competes on Doublet. Together, against considerable odds, they won at Burghley in 1971*

can ride them over the open Norfolk fields or across the wind-swept Scottish moors. Princess Anne has always been the speed merchant of the family and though the Queen enjoys the occasional gallop with her daughter across the stubble fields of Sandringham, Princess Anne is always the winner. At Balmoral the quiet hacks on Benbow are too sedate and pedestrian to appeal to her daughter.

One of the annual 'unofficial' fixtures in the royal sporting calendar takes place during the week of Royal Ascot, when the Queen and her guests at Windsor Castle take part in the early morning gallops round the course, before returning for a late breakfast. In recent years Princess Anne has been the regular winner of these as well.

Windsor is the setting for Prince Philip's two principal horsey activities, polo and competition driving. He started to play polo after the war as a way of sharing in his wife's interests in horses. Under the tuition of his uncle, Lord Louis Mountbatten, he made rapid progress and soon found that the game perfectly suited his love of violent exercise and his strongly competitive spirit.

He soon set about establishing his own string of highly trained ponies at Windsor where he played regularly on Smith's Lawn and captained the Windsor polo team until

1971. Polo ponies have to be supple, quick to respond to the rider and easily manoeuvrable; they also have to be fast on the straight.

This last characteristic was certainly true of Betaway, which was probably Prince Philip's best-known polo pony. She was the granddaughter of the Derby winner Hyperion and this thoroughbred blood made her unbeatable in a straight chase for the ball.

Prince Philip also had several Argentinian bred ponies which are usually cross-breeds, and though slightly slower than the thoroughbred ponies they tend to be faster on the turn and generally better suited to the game. Noche Dia was one such Argentinian pony, which Prince Philip considered to be one of his best. Alert and responsive, she had a tranquil, co-operative nature which proved to be invaluable in testing games. When all Prince Philip's attention had to be directed on the game, he could almost let the mare take care of herself.

Most of Prince Philip's English ponies were bred at the Royal Stud at Sandringham. Amongst them Bullseye, Global and Lightning were somewhat enigmatic when it came to polo. Bullseye seemed to be an absolute dead loss in her first year and then miraculously transformed the following season to become one of Prince Philip's most enthusiastic ponies. Lightning was a bright chestnut mare who discovered a way of augmenting her strict diet with bedding straw, in spite of wearing a heavy leather muzzle, and had the endearing habit of trying to bite her rider whenever he was about to mount her. On the field she was one of the Prince's fastest ponies, but there again she would work herself up into a 'tizzy' and go haywire when other ponies were about, which altogether made her quite a handful to manage during a game.

In 1971 Prince Philip played polo for the last time. He had always maintained that he would give up the game when he was fifty and a recurring wrist injury ensured that he did. But he was fortunate that another, equally demanding sport was at his disposal, and he dismounted from the polo saddle only to step just as confidently into the driving seat of a competition driving carriage.

Until the early seventies competition driving was an exclusively European sport, but when one of the delegates to the Fédération Equestre Internationale, of which Prince Philip was president, suggested that some rules ought to be laid down for this sport, the seeds of the idea were sown in his head.

He was ideally situated to take up the sport, having the horses and carriages of the Royal Mews at his disposal. He started learning how to drive a single horse to begin with, but within the space of two years he was competing in the most difficult and demanding four-in-hand competitions.

The international competitions in which he competes are based on the three-day events in which Princess Anne has made such a name for herself. There are marks awarded for presentation and dressage, there are cross-country courses to be negotiated with skill and daring and there are obstacle courses which involve steering the horses and carriage between markers against the clock.

Prince Philip has miniature practice courses at Windsor and Sandringham and he regularly competes at Smith's Lawn and at the Windsor Horse Show. He drives Windsor Greys, Cleveland Bays and Haflingers as well as other horses from the Royal Mews and his vehicles range from large drags, or coaches, to small pony landaus. The Prince reckons that this sport should keep him content for another ten years, before he has to look around for something else to do.

Above *Edward began to hunt while at university. He was renowned for his daring, though perhaps less skilful than his brother George*

Above right *The Prince of Wales was finally persuaded to give up point-to-point racing. Here he resaddles after a second fall in one race*

Of course his connection with polo has not completely disappeared since he has a vicarious interest in watching Prince Charles's progress and development. Prince Charles learned to ride on a faithful old pony called William, but he got his first taste of polo on one of his father's ponies called San Quanina, while he was still at school. He played polo for Cambridge and captained the Young England Team against Young America in 1972, when he scored a goal. However, it was not until after leaving the Navy, that he could become fully involved with a polo season. However, he made such rapid progress that year that a special meeting of the Hurl-

ingham Polo Association had to be called to raise his handicap from two to three.

His coach, who is one of the few men allowed to swear at him, reckons that he has more natural ability than even his father. His technique is almost faultless, he has great positional strength and he is fearless. His one problem is that his play lacks the ruthless aggression that would make him a top-class player; he is essentially too kind to his ponies. In addition with fewer than ten ponies in his string, experts feel that he lacks the quality of mounts which are required by international-class players.

However, polo ponies cost over three thousand pounds each and they have to be changed frequently, since the strain on them is so great. In fact one of Prince Charles's ponies died during a game in 1978. So it is unlikely that the Prince will ever feel justified in spending more money than he does at present on what is after all a pastime.

Since leaving the Navy he has taken up two of the sports favoured by the previous Prince of Wales, hunting and cross-country riding. He hunts with all the leading packs in the country including the Belvoir, the Quorn and the Cotswold, although this has been heavily criticised by opponents of hunting. He has stated that he would be prepared to give up the sport if ever he felt the majority of the people wished him to.

He usually rides horses from the royal stables like Candlewick, on which he also com-

peted at the Royal Windsor Horse Show in 1979. The same horses are used in cross-country riding, which is similar to hunting, but without the fox. Like his great-uncle, Prince Charles has had his fair share of falls, but like his great-uncle, too he laughs these off, commenting after two falls on the same day in Leicestershire: 'Good practice for parachute jumping.' He now captains two teams of his own, the Duke of Cornwall's Chasers and the Earl of Chester's Chasers.

His most recent undertaking has also followed the footsteps of his great-uncle, steeplechasing. He has tried his hand at driving vehicles ranging from landaus to trotters, although his experiences with the latter looked distinctly uncomfortable when he had a go on a trotting rig on a friend's estate near Fife. Although he does not seem set to overtake his father in that sport, just yet, it will not be long before he has reached his standard on the polo field, in spite of being hampered by his ponies.

It might take Prince Charles rather longer to emulate his sister's success as an international event rider and show jumper. Princess Anne combines her mother's instinctive understanding of horses with her father's aggressive will to win, a combination which made her Individual European Champion in 1971 and BBC Sports Personality of the Year.

Like Prince Charles, she also began to ride on William, whom she could manage on her own by the time she was seven. The first pony which she could really call her own was High Jinks, a nice-looking brown gelding with a striped face, which accompanied her when she went away to boarding school, and on whom she had her first taste of success in pony club rallies. In 1963 she won a small one-day event organised for young riders at Windsor, and in the following year she and Jinks were part of the winning team from Benenden that took away the Combined Training Cup.

Like most family ponies, High Jinks lived outside for most of the year, only coming in to his stable on the coldest winter nights. Prince Andrew's hardy little Shetland pony Valkyrie, followed the same régime. Anne acquired her

riding skills like any other schoolgirl. There were no special privileges. She was expected to take care of her pony and his tack like anyone else and when it came to tuition she had to take her turn with the rest.

It was while she was at school that her instructor suggested that she might consider taking up event riding, which combined all the necessities of high standards of training for the show ring with the excitement and skill of cross-country riding. By the time she left school, Princess Anne and High Jinks had made quite a name for themselves in the junior competitions, but these were nothing like as demanding as the senior competitions to which she aspired.

She was fortunate in obtaining the help of a trainer as proficient as Alison Oliver, but a good share of the success must go to her own hard work and determination.

Her first horse, Purple Star, was completely inexperienced in eventing, yet through her efforts she enabled him to give some impressive performances, which in turn raised her own standard.

Purple Star was followed by the now famous Doublet, which had been bred originally as a polo pony for Prince Philip, before it was found that he was too big. Alison Oliver had her work cut out to transform this unpredictable and temperamental horse into the champion it later became, and when Princess Anne and Doublet qualified to take part in the Badminton three-day event in 1971 there were many who doubted whether either

Left *Charles plays polo at Smith's Lawn, now enjoying the sport which his father favoured for so many years*
Below *The Duke of Edinburgh steers his Haflinger ponies around the obstacle course at the Windsor Horse Show*

clusion in the British team for the Olympic three-day event seem very likely, but Doublet pulled a tendon which unfortunately put them out of the running.

In the autumn of 1972 the princess acquired a grade A jumper called Goodwill, and this was the horse on which she has principally competed ever since. In 1973 they came eighth at Badminton, in 1976 they competed in the British team in the Olympic Games in Montreal and they competed again at Badminton in 1978 and 1979.

As the friendship between Princess Anne and Mark Phillips deepened they started to share horses. In 1972, the Princess lent the Queen's horse Columbus to Mark Phillips, after she had found him too much to handle herself, and he too fell off. A year after their wedding though, he had got the measure of the horse and together they came first at Badminton. Since then Columbus has gone on to win many other competitions.

Captain Phillips's own horses have been highly successful too. A year after winning Badminton in 1971 he and Great Ovation came first again and these brilliant successes have been followed in recent years with horses like Lauriman.

horse or rider were really experienced enough to compete. The doubts were confounded when they finished fifth out of forty. The winners were a young army officer named Mark Phillips and his horse Great Ovation.

There were still doubts about the Princess and Doublet when they competed in the Burghley event later that year, and these increased when it was learnt that Princess Anne was to have an operation only six weeks before the competition. The story of how she struggled to get fit and the way in which she won is now well known, but it was a victory achieved against significant odds by both horse and rider.

The success at Burghley made their in-

Left *The Queen proudly leads her filly Carrozza from the course. Carrozza and her jockey, Lester Piggott have just won the Oaks at the 1957 Derby*

THE SPORT OF KINGS

*H*er Majesty the Queen's absorbing interest in horses is as familiar to her subjects as her love of that peculiar, little fox-faced dog, the Welsh corgi—indeed Her Majesty's critics have seldom failed to censure her frequent and undisguised attendance at race meetings. Among the racing fraternity, however, the Queen is acknowledged and respected as one of the leading authorities on the breeding and training of race horses in the country.

In this she is following a royal line that stretches back through her ancestors to the Plantagenet kings of the Middle Ages. Several of Her Majesty's predecessors were very active in trying to improve the breeding of English horses. Horses were imported from abroad throughout the thirteenth, fourteenth and fifteenth centuries and Henry VIII, the father of the Queen's namesake, introduced several laws specifically designed to eliminate the strains of horses that were not likely to answer 'the needs of the country'. These laws reflected a close, personal knowledge of horse breeding and the necessity of improving national bloodstock. And the result of King Henry's concern was the probable establishment of the first royal stud.

Horse racing itself had taken place spasmodically for hundreds of years before the establishment of the Sport of Kings at the beginning of the seventeenth century. There is evidence that the Romans held horse races at Wetherby in the third century A.D. Tournaments on horseback were popular events in the Middle Ages and it is likely that these included races over specified distances; although as far as Edward II was concerned this was definitely not the Sport of Kings. He marked his disapproval of these contests in

banning tournaments due to be held at 'Novum Mercatum' (Newmarket) in 1309 and 1313.

It was not until 1603 that horse racing became established as a sport in its own right in England, and then ironically, the sport which has been so closely associated with the English ever since, was imported from Scotland. James VI of Scotland and I of England may have been one of the least competent of royal horsemen — he had to be strapped into his saddle to prevent him falling off — but what he lacked in expertise he made up for in enthusiasm. And though the King's sporting interests lay in hunting, his noble subjects were passionately devoted to horse racing.

The King favoured Newmarket Heath as a hunting centre and the court which followed him there established their own favourite sport on the now famous Norfolk turf. His eldest son, later Charles I, was the first king to take a close interest in racing. During his reign regular meetings were established at Newmarket which rapidly became the racing Mecca of the country. In 1634 the Golden Cup is first mentioned as a prize, and other trophies were introduced as a result of royal enthusiasm and patronage. To begin with it appears that races were only held between two horses, with eliminating rounds taking the form of heats, though later six or more horses competed.

Laws passed by the Commonwealth prohibited racing along with many other entertainments and brought about the dispersal of the royal studs. This last act though, proved to be a positive advantage to the sport, for it enabled breeders throughout the country to acquire strains of imported breeds which

would otherwise have been barred to them. Among these strains were the offspring of two Arab stallions, Markham Arabian and White Turk, which had been imported by James I, but which were thought little of by the acknowledged experts in horseflesh. Crossed with existing native breeds they now established the first in the line that led to the great English thoroughbreds.

Charles II, played a very active part in re-establishing racing after the Restoration. He took upon himself the position of unofficial umpire and steward in many races at Newmarket. He also established the nerve-racking practice of galloping alongside the competitors during the closing stages of the race, a habit quickly adopted by his followers. Perhaps most importantly he was instrumental in creating the first rules of racing.

By the time William of Orange ascended the throne in 1689 racing was firmly established in England. The new King adopted the sport almost as soon as he arrived in the country. But his most lasting connection with the Turf was the establishment of the Royal Stud at Hampton Court, where it remained for two hundred years before being transferred to Sandringham.

During William III's reign, too, the reputation of British bloodstock on the continent was advanced by gifts of horses made by the King to foreign heads of state, including Louis XIV and the kings of Sweden and Prussia. The traffic in horses which until then had been one-way now began to swing in the opposite direction.

English bloodstock and racing in general probably owes more to King William's successor than to any other single monarch.

Queen Anne, who was described as having the outside of a horse and the inside of a man, was devoted to hunting and racing. She and her husband, Prince George of Denmark, were both generous and enthusiastic patrons of the Turf. They gave gold plates and cups to be raced for, they gave large sums of money to promote racing and they showed keen interest in the breeding of racehorses.

In conjunction with her trainer, William Frampton, who had the distinction of serving four monarchs in this capacity, she continued to import eastern stallions for the royal studs and one of these, known as the Darley Arabian, became one of the most important sires in the history of racing.

The horse was named after the British consul in Aleppo who had negotiated its purchase from the local sheik. After the deal had been completed and the agreed price of three hundred sovereigns had been paid, the sheik had refused to allow the consul to take the horse away. The animal was eventually secured by a group of British sailors who overpowered its guards and smuggled it out to their ship by night. Their efforts were certainly well rewarded though, because the Darley Arabian became one of the three priceless horses that founded the thoroughbred.

Queen Anne was also responsible for encouraging the spread of racing throughout the kingdom. Until her reign Newmarket had been the sole national meeting, but she inaugurated Royal Ascot, which was near her home at Windsor, and also sent her horses to race at far away York, where her last winner, Star, galloped home at the head of the field only a few days before her death.

In spite of the total indifference to racing

shown by the first three Georges, the sport continued to flourish, thanks largely to the breeding legacy they inherited. George II's second son, the Duke of Cumberland took a very different attitude to his relations on the throne. Apart from being one of the founder members of the Jockey Club, he bred Eclipse, the most famous horse of the eighteenth century, and Herod, which together with Match-em is one of the direct ancestors of all the thoroughbred racehorses in the world today.

Eclipse was a remarkable animal and the legend he created is commemorated by a plaque in Windsor Great Park which marks the paddock in which he was foaled. In his first public race he won the first heat so convincingly that his owner, who was then a Colonel O'Kelly, rashly offered to place the entries in the final race, at any price. His bold pronoun-cement: 'Eclipse first, the rest nowhere', was handsomely confirmed when, living up to his name, the horse romped home far ahead of the rest of the field. By the time that Eclipse retired he had won all eighteen of the record-ed races he entered, including eleven King's Plates, and not once had any of his jockeys needed to goad him on with either the whip or spurs.

The neglect of racing by his immediate predecessors evidently had little influence on the Prince Regent whose staggering debts were largely accounted for by his passion for the sport. At the time of his greatest financial embarrassment he had twenty-five horses training at New-market and the annual upkeep of his racing stables alone amounted to over thirty-one thousand pounds.

However, he enjoyed his fair share of success as well, with one hundred and seven wins in the first seven years of the nineteenth century, and a total of three hundred and thirteen wins over a period of twenty years.

In spite of her love of horses, Queen Victoria never showed any great interest in racing and the only occasion when she attended a race meeting away from Ascot was a visit to watch the Derby run at Epsom in 1840. She maintained the Royal Stud at Hampton Court however, and this continued to breed some of the finest horses in the country. But the real racing enthusiast in the family was her eldest son who later became Edward VII.

As Prince of Wales he registered his racing colours with the Jockey Club in 1875 and these were essentially the same as those still worn by the Queen's jockey today, namely purple body, scarlet sleeves and black velvet cap with a gold tassel.

Prince Edward took a keen interest in breeding horses as well as in owning them. In 1887 his trainer John Porter bought a mare named Perdita II who was to become the dam of some of the Prince's finest winners, among them Florizel II, Persimmon and Diamond Jubilee.

Florizel II won a total of seven thousand eight hundred and fifty-eight pounds in stake money for his owner. This included notable victories in the Gold Vase at Ascot, the Goodwood Cup and the Newmarket's Jockey Club Cup. While at stud he sired a Derby winner named Volodyovski; a winner of the St. Ledger called Doricles; and the Two Thousand Guineas winner, Vedas.

Florizel II's famous full-brother Persimmon won two races in 1895. In 1896 he won the Derby, the St. Ledger, and the Jockey Club Stakes, and the following year he won the Ascot Gold Cup and the Eclipse Stakes at Sandown Park. Altogether Persimmon won over thirty-four thousand pounds, though his ninety-seven winning offspring together netted in excess of two hundred and thirty-two thousand pounds.

In 1900 the remarkable Diamond Jubilee took the Two Thousand Guineas, the Newmarket Stakes, the Derby, the Eclipse Stakes and the St. Ledger, thus winning the coveted triple crown, while His Royal Highness's steeplechaser, Ambush II, won the Grand National.

Nine years later the King had an equally successful season, this time with another famous horse called Minoru which won the Greenham Stakes, the Two Thousand Guineas, the Derby, the St. James's Palace Stakes at Ascot, the Surrey Stakes at Goodwood and the Newmarket Free Handicap.

King Edward's final victory came on the day of his death the following year. In spite of the King's rapidly deteriorating health, Buckingham Palace had ordered that his filly Witch of the Air should still run at Kempton Park. The news of her victory and the exciting finish, in which she overhauled and beat the favourite Queen Tii by a neck, reached the King at about five o'clock on 6 May. Less than seven hours later he died, bringing to an end a life which had firmly established racing as the Sport of Kings.

At Sandringham Edward VII left behind him some of the finest bloodstock in the country, which was inherited by his son and heir, King George V. The great weathered-bronze statue of Persimmon which still stands in front of the Sandringham Stud on the Anmer Road is a constant reminder of his owner's devotion to the English thoroughbred.

The Queen's grandfather was perhaps more interested in the breeding of racehorses than

The daredevil George IV drives to Ascot with a 'lady of quality'

anyone in the royal family since the Duke of Cumberland. During the 1920's and 1930's the royal studs at Sandringham and nearby Wolferton produced outstanding horses like Scuttle, which won the Two Thousand Guineas in 1928, and incidentally made George V the first reigning monarch to breed and own a classic winner, Weather Vane, which won the Royal Hunt Cup and Limelight, who was the winner of the Hardwicke Stakes in 1933.

Undoubtedly His Majesty's most successful horse was the dark brown stallion Friar Marcus, which was also bred at Sandringham. As a two-year-old he ran on five occasions and was never beaten in races like the Goodwood Prince of Wales Stakes, the Middle Park Plate and the Rous Memorial Stakes. The following year he added the Great Eastern Railway Handicap and the Queensbury Handicap to his tally of victories, while as a four-year-old he won the Crawford Handicap and the Chesterfield Handicap.

When Friar Marcus returned to the royal stud it was assumed that as a sprinter himself he would sire other sprinters, but the King always maintained that the horse came from good staying stock, and the victory (in the St. Ledger) of his offspring Braham, which belonged to the Aga Khan, proved this point convincingly.

Anmer was another of the King's horses to catch the public eye, though for rather different reasons. This was the King's entry in the 1913 Derby. Emily Davison, a suffragette, ran out from the rails as the horses were rounding Tattenham Corner and flung herself under their hooves. Anmer was brought down and Miss Davison was killed, though miraculously neither the horse nor its jockey, Herbert Jones, was seriously injured.

King George V must still have been very much in the spectators' minds when the horse which had foaled in his Jubilee Year, and which was named Jubilee after it, won the Molyneux Stakes at the Liverpool Spring Meeting at the start of his son's Coronation year. This was Jubilee's first race and the first winner in a race run under Jockey Club rules for King George VI.

George VI was never a great racing enthusiast and had to be persuaded to attend race meetings by his wife and elder daughter. But he was genuinely interested in the royal racing stables and was as pleased as any of the family whenever a royal horse won. He was also aware of Princess Elizabeth's obvious interest in horses from an early age, and she was once taken by her father to watch two of his most successful wartime horses, Big Game and Sun Chariot, training before the Derby and the Oaks in 1942. Both these horses had in fact been leased to the King for their racing careers from the National Stud, a practice which continued into his daughter's reign. As two-year-olds neither horse had ever been beaten, and in 1942 they won four of the five classic races for the King, Big Game winning the Two Thousand Guineas and Sun Chariot winning the One Thousand Guineas, the Oaks and the St. Ledger.

This outstanding achievement at a time of great national hardship established King George VI as the first reigning monarch in the history of the Turf to head the list of winning owners. In addition he was the first man to win four classics with two horses in the same year. In the middle of the war this combination of the King and horses from the National Stud was a perfect symbol of national unity.

The immediate post war years saw further royal victories. In 1946 the temperamental filly Hypericum provided a spectacular performance in the One Thousand Guineas at Newmarket. As the runners were lining up at the start she charged the tapes, which swept off her jockey, Doug Smith, and proceeded to gallop away in the general direction of her stable. She was finally caught by the driver of the Newmarket fire engine and was united with her jockey and the rest of the field after an interlude of a quarter of an hour. Not content with this display of bravado, however, Hypericum had the audacity to outstay the favourite and gallop up the rising ground to the finish a clear winner.

In the following year Princess Elizabeth married Lieutenant Philip Mountbatten and received, along with thousands of other wedding gifts, a racehorse, named Astrakhan, from the Aga Khan. Astrakhan eventually won a few minor races, but not before the Princess's colours had been carried to victory on the steeplechaser, Monaveen.

Elizabeth's principal racing interests have always been on the flat, but her career as a winning owner began with the joint ownership of Monaveen which she shared with her mother.

This partnership had been instigated by one of the most popular and likeable figures in the National Hunt world, the leading amateur jockey Lord Mildmay. He had suggested to the Queen over dinner one evening during the Ascot week that she might enjoy owning a steeplechaser. The idea and the manner in which it was put to her intrigued the Queen so much that she promptly suggested to her daughter that they might go into the project together. As a result the royal ladies acquired Monaveen, who immediately repaid their interest by winning four steeplechases that season, and went on to come fifth in the 1950 Grand National. After Monaveen's sad death at Hurst Park, however, it was agreed that the Queen should stick with the steeplechasers while her daughter concentrated on her first love, the flat.

Between King George VI's death and his funeral in 1952, all racing was suspended, but once it started again the tide of royal successes continued. In the Ascot meeting of that year Gay Time, which had just been leased to the Queen from the National Stud, gave her the first win of her reign, but it was the prospect of a royal win in the Derby four days after the Coronation the following year which really excited the nation.

The cause of this excited anticipation was a handsome chestnut called Aureole. The Queen had named the horse herself. His dam was Angelola who had been named after a

Left *The Queen appears in public at the races with little reserve. At the 1978 Derby she was greeted unexpectedly by a 'bunny'*

Opposite page *Traditionally the royal family rides around the course before breakfast during Royal Ascot week*

Below *'If it were not for my Archbishop of Canterbury I should be off in my plane to Longchamps every Sunday.' The Queen is seen here with the Princess Royal at the Oaks in 1962*

sculpture by the Italian master Donatello. Since many of his carvings of saints featured haloes around their brows, the name Aureole was chosen for Angelola's colt, though like Hyperion's daughters Sun Chariot and Hypericum, he was to show few saintly virtues.

Aureole had looked promising right from the start of his career, and after his volatile temperament had been slightly curbed by patient trainers, he ran well in the Two Thousand Guineas in 1953, and then came home an easy winner in the Lingfield Trail for the Derby. The Queen was clearly thrilled at the prospect that Aureole might give her her first Derby victory, and a story is told that on the morning of the Coronation itself she was asked if all was well only to give the answer: 'Oh yes, the Captain has just rung to say that Aureole went really well.'

Four days later at Epsom he ran well too, though not quite well enough to run home ahead of Pinza, ridden by the champion jockey Sir Gordon Richards, whose knighthood had been announced on the morning of the Coronation.

However, Aureole's uneasy temperament still remained an obstacle to consistent success and the Queen, always willing to try new and unorthodox training methods, suggested asking a leading London neurologist, Dr. Charles Brook, to treat her favourite, but exceedingly difficult horse. Dr. Brook's technique though simple had proved surprisingly successful with other horses and within a few sessions of his literally laying hands on Aureole, the horse had grown noticeably more placid.

Luckily this treatment did nothing to diminish Aureole's will to win, and in his final season, 1954, he won the Hardwicke Stakes, the Coronation Cup and the King George VI and Queen Elizabeth Stakes. Though even in this last race his nerves almost spelt disaster. As Eph Smith was riding him up to the start, Aureole was startled by an umbrella suddenly opened in the crowd. The horse reared and

threw his jockey from his back. With great presence of mind Eph Smith grabbed a handful of grass and the horse came meekly over to him. He remounted and together they went on to win the race.

There were other successes for the Queen that year as well, and at the end of the season she headed the list of winning owners for the first time. Aureole retired to the Wolferton Stud at the end of 1954, becoming champion sire twice in the next twenty years, and producing offspring that would win in excess of one million pounds.

Three years later the Queen was again winning owner, this time through the efforts of her filly Almeria who won the Ribblesdale Stakes at Royal Ascot, the Eclipse Stakes at Sandown Park, the Yorkshire Oaks at York and the Park Hill Stakes at Doncaster. Carrozza, ridden by Lester Piggott, also won the Oaks that year.

And so the royal victories continued throughout the 1950's. In 1958 Doutelle and Almeria finished second and third respectively in the King George VI and Queen Elizabeth Stakes, Pall Mall won the Two Thousand Guineas, and Agreement the Doncaster Cup and the Chester Cup, Above Suspicion won the St. James's Palace Stakes and Pindari, leased from the National Stud, won the Great Voltigeur Stakes at York.

After 1960, however, the royal stud went into a decline and there was an evident need for an injection of new blood. The victory of Canisbee in the Eclipse Stakes in 1965 proved to be the major highlight in an otherwise disappointing period, but during that time the foundations were being laid for a new generation of royal champions.

It was decided to split the Queen's horses between the establishments of two well-known trainers. Some were to go to Ian Balding's stables at Kingsclere in Hampshire, while the others were to be sent to Dick Hern's at West Ilsley in Berkshire. The brood mares, as always, were to be kept at Sandringham and Wolferton, though later the Queen bought another stud at Polhampton in Hampshire which was to be used by the foals once they had been weaned. The division

Above *Prince Charles smiles after his first flat race. Riding an American horse, Long Wharf, he came in second at Plumpton, March 1980*

Opposite page *The Queen Mother is delighted too. Sunnyboy has just won at Ascot, bringing her winning total of races to 300. 1976*

Below right *The Queen gives another of her horses, Highclere, an affectionate pat. 1977*

between the two racing stables now takes place when the horses are a year old.

In the 1970's the Queen's two outstanding horses were Highclere and Dunfermline. Highclere was born at the home of the father of the Queen's racing manager, Lord Porchester, and was named after it. A large rich bay filly, she was always looked upon as a promising three-year-old and this proved to be exactly the case. After a couple of races as a two-year-old she was entered for the One Thousand Guineas in 1974 without having previously raced that year. Probably as a result of this she started the race seventh in the betting list. However, the faith of her trainer, Dick Hern, and her jockey, Joe Mercer, paid off and in a thrilling photo finish she won from her rival Polygamy by a matter of inches.

Probably Highclere's greatest triumph came in France though, where against a field of twenty-one top-class opponents she won the Prix de Diane by a comfortable two

lengths which sent the French crowd into uncharacteristic jubilation at this English royal victory. It was a tremendous triumph for the Queen who had shown such a close interest in the breeding and racing of her horses since coming to the throne. And by this win Highclere also made racing history, becoming the first filly to win both the One Thousand Guineas and the Prix de Diane, and also becoming the greatest money-winning filly ever bred in the British Isles.

To the Queen racing is as important as it has always been. Talking to her trainers and jockeys, mixing with other enthusiasts, sharing in the thrills and disappointments of the races themselves, the Queen comes as close as she ever can to being treated as an equal. Her lifelong love of horses and her innate skill with them have bred a deep-seated bond between the owner and her racehorses, which is one of the most satisfying and rewarding pleasures she enjoys.

Perhaps as a second choice to a life in the country with lots of dogs and horses, the Queen might have chosen a career as a full-time breeder and trainer of racehorses. She has certainly shown herself to be remarkably proficient in the little time that her present public duties allow her. And her attachment to the Turf is undeniable, as she once observed: 'If it were not for my Archbishop of Canterbury, I should be off in my plane to Longchamps every Sunday.'

The Queen and Prince Philip examine their stock at Balmoral

ROYAL ANIMALS OF FARM AND FIELD

*O*n 2 February, 1979, nineteen hinds from the herd of red deer from Balmoral arrived at Windsor to be released into a re-established deer park in the north of Windsor Great Park. The idea was the brain-child of the Ranger of Windsor Great Park, Prince Philip, and in his action he was effectively turning the clock back nearly one thousand years.

Until recent times, venison was a crucial part of the royal diet. In the Middle Ages, and no doubt for centuries before that, the great forests of England were a vital source of food for the king and his court. The herds of deer that roamed in what later became the royal hunting parks were systematically culled to provide meat for the royal table, while care was taken to leave a sufficiently large breeding herd to maintain stocks. And this is exactly the policy that is in operation at Balmoral today, although neither the deer there, nor those at Windsor, form an essential part of the diet of the modern royal family or their guests. Venison is unusual and it's tasty, so they like eating it.

Clearly, modern deer-stalking is the occupation of the sportsman as opposed to that of the hunter, and the great deer hunts of the Middle Ages had to be conducted on a far less 'sportsmanlike' basis in order to ensure that the required amount of food was obtained. Instead of individual hunters pursuing their own quarry over miles of forest and moor, they were carefully positioned by the Chief Hunter and the deer were then driven towards them by a curving line of beaters, very much as pheasant shoots are conducted today. In consequence the margin of error in the firing of bows and arrows was minimised and the hunters had the satisfaction of both killing their prey and providing food for the king's larders. Likewise, poachers more than simply spoilt the king's hunting, they severely interfered with the rearing of his most important food supply. Deer in the medieval forests were considered as livestock, and only when other sources of meat superseded venison did they become 'game'.

The most important royal hunting reserve was Windsor Forest, which at times spread far enough to encompass the whole of Surrey. During the last two hundred years its boundaries have gradually receded to those which exist today. Yet even at the beginning of the Second World War there was still a vast herd of deer roaming in Windsor Great Park, and in 1941 the King directed that they should be rounded up and slaughtered to make way for wartime agricultural needs, leaving a small breeding herd to maintain the stock. The deer introduced in 1979 will replace those of forty years ago.

One curious feature of the improved agricultural methods which swept through the country in the eighteenth century was the practice of stall-feeding deer. As late as 1822 there is a reference to stall-fed deer at one of the royal farms near Hampton Court, an example of the traditional royal attitude to deer taken to its logical conclusion. There are no stall-fed deer on farms today, but for that matter there is no reason why there should not be. If there is a sudden demand for venison, perhaps one of the royal farms will pioneer the technique?

Royal breeders have led the field in introducing new strains of livestock into agriculture just as much as they have been responsible for improving more glamorous animals like horses and dogs. And of all the royal farmers George III, *Farmer George,* made the greatest contribution, the Merino sheep.

Traditionally, wool has been one of the greatest British exports. Today the Lord Chancellor still sits on the woolsack, a symbol of the importance played by wool in establishing our trading superiority throughout the world. However, at the beginning of the eighteenth century, when Britain was reaching her trading heights, there was intense interest in the Merino sheep of Spain, which for hundreds of years had been producing some of the finest wool in the world.

The Merinos were the exclusive property of certain Spanish nobles, notably the king, and their export were strictly prohibited. However, in the second half of the eighteenth century two small flocks were sent to Saxony and France, where they made significant improvements to the native stock. Hearing of these successes, George III was determined to obtain some Merinos himself.

The process involved much cloak and dagger work, bribing Spanish shepherds and smuggling a few sheep at a time through Portugal and eventually by ship to England, where they were sent to the King's farm at Kew. But over a period of five years the King acquired fourteen Merino rams and seventy-three ewes, only to find that the King of Spain made him a special gift of forty of his best sheep in 1791.

After the success of bringing the sheep to England, the project looked doomed to failure in its early years, as gradually the sheep succumbed to the harsher English climate. They suffered from lung worm, scab, footrot and other afflictions that included 'red water', 'mad staggers' and 'flounder in the liver'. Careful husbandry and the timely arrival of nearly fifteen thousand prime Merinos from war-torn Spain saved the flock and ensured the supply of good breeding stock to be integrated with native sheep. But, more importantly, it guaranteed supplies to the new pastures in the rapidly developing colonies on the other side of the world. The first Merinos landed in Sydney in 1805 and from these half dozen sprang the present Australian sheep industry.

The climate in Australia was better suited to the Merino than that in England and when the sheep were later introduced to South Africa and New Zealand, the results were equally promising. George III may not have introduced a sheep which was an outstanding success in Britain, but the wealth of three of his colonies was directly based on this act of foresight and imagination.

A further attempt to develop the British wool trade was made by Queen Victoria and Prince Albert, though this never got much above the level of a cottage industry. When she came to the throne, the new Queen found that among the other animals living in Windsor Great Park there were a flock of Cashmere goats which had descended from a pair given to George IV. The process of collecting and spinning the wonderfully soft wool is time-consuming and laborious, even a mature Cashmere billy-goat will not produce more than four ounces of wool a year but, nevertheless, the idea seized the Queen's imagination and for thirty years Cashmere garments from Windsor were all the rage.

Right *The Queen talks with farm girls on the Sandringham estate during the harvest of 1943*
Below *Young Prince Charles accidentally lets go of the rope, Balmoral 1957*

Society ladies used to help sort out the wool from the Queen's goats and at its peak there were more than one thousand people occupied in producing the few garments that were made. A fresh arrival of goats from India helped sustain the herd for a further forty years, but in 1936 it was dispersed and most of the goats were transferred to the London Zoo, so ending the only royal textile industry in Britain.

Today the royal farms have to be commercially viable and, thanks to the great interest taken in them by their owners, for the most part they are. However, there are still certain favourite breeds that remain on the farm primarily through personal sentiment rather than sound agricultural management, and

the best-known of these is the herd of Jersey cattle at Windsor.

There have been several hints made to the Queen that the Jerseys should be replaced by higher-yielding Friesians, but she will hear nothing of it. She is proud of the herd's successes in agricultural shows over many years, especially as most of the leading specimens were bred on her own farms. She also shows as much interest in their breeding and their pedigrees as she does in her racing bloodstock, which is only natural in a herd inherited from her great-great-grandmother Queen Victoria. And like many English thoroughbreds, animals from the Windsor Jersey herd have been sent all over the world, from Iran to Brazil, to help establish new dairy herds or strengthen existing ones.

There are also Hereford, Friesian and Ayrshire cattle on the Windsor estate, the Ayrshire herd being installed in the final year of the Queen's father's reign. But the Jerseys are still the oldest and most prestigious of the herds.

Until 1973 they were milked in Prince Albert's cowshed, a masterpiece of Victorian design and elaborate tiled decoration. The dairy is still used, not for milking cattle, but for preparing special milk, cream and cream cheese for the royal table. Three times a week milk from the Royal Dairy Farm, Windsor, is delivered to Buckingham Palace in bottles stamped with a crown and the initials ER II. The cream and cream cheese are sent to London whenever they are required.

Balmoral is the home of a herd of traditional, shaggy Highland cattle, but these form only a small part of the cattle population of the estate. The principal breeds are

Far left *The dairy at Windsor was built by Queen Victoria and provided fresh milk daily*
Left *Princess Anne seems charmed by this goat*
Below left *Prince Andrew makes overtures to an Australian steer*
Below *Charles inspects the shires!*

Galloway and Luing cattle which are bred for beef. Both herds fulfil the two essential criteria for all the royal farms, they are commercially successful and they also provide meat for the household. This policy makes the royal farms as self-sufficient as the deer parks of hundreds of years ago.

Economy also forced the dispersal of the famous pedigree herd of Red Poll cattle which were reared at Sandringham until 1959. They have since been replaced by three herds of blue-grey cattle and two herds of Herefords crossed with Friesians. And in the most recent of the royal farming enterprises, Gatcombe, Captain Phillips was presented with an astonishing hotch-potch of cattle when he took over the estate. However, he has started to rationalise his herd and, with luck, will end up with about one hundred and twenty beef cows, made up of some Hereford crossed with Friesians, some blue-greys and a few French Charolais cows.

Among the sheep on the royal farms there is a small intriguing herd of Soay sheep at Balmoral, which are kept solely to provide tender mutton for the royal family and their guests. These sheep have an interesting history, representing as they do the last specimens of a type of prehistoric sheep which were once common throughout Europe.

The ones at Balmoral originated from a semi-wild herd that lived on the island of Soay in the Outer Hebrides. When the island sheep were brought to the mainland they flourished and as a consequence they were exported to Europe and North America. Some eventually found their way to Balmoral, where they are still allowed to live in a semi-wild state.

Further north in Caithness the Queen Mother keeps a herd of prize-winning North Country Cheviot sheep on her little farm attached to the Castle of Mey. Like her daughter, the Queen Mother takes an intense interest and pride in her farm animals. In 1977 a North Country Cheviot ram, in which she had a joint share, won first prize at the Royal Highland Show as male and overall breed champion and a year later the same animal won the same event. In 1978 she also showed a tup lamb at the Royal Highland Show and this again came first in its class. But her interest in livestock is not wholly partisan. Her Majesty the Queen Mother is patron of the Aberdeen Angus Society, of which she has a pedigree herd of twenty-five cows, and she is also an Honorary Life Member of the Royal Agricultural Society.

Pigs have been grubbing about in Windsor Great Park for almost as long as there have been deer there. There is a record of grazing rights for fifty hogs in part of the royal estate which was noted in the Domesday Book in the eleventh century, and pigs have been bred at Windsor ever since.

Today they are housed in modern buildings and look very different from their medieval ancestors, thanks largely to the efforts of

Prince Albert. Throughout his life in England he regularly exhibited his Windsor pigs at local and national agricultural shows, so that they eventually became recognised as a distinct breed, Prince Albert's Windsor Breed. In fact, they were probably similar to the present-day Large White. There is no denying their success, though, and they made an important contribution to the farming finances of the estate during his lifetime.

Today the pig herd is a purely commercial unit relying on a cross of Landrace boars with Large White sows, which has shown a steady improvement in the number of litters and the number of piglets in each litter over the last ten years,

The royal farms run successfully and royal livestock win prizes at agricultural shows as a result of the same enthusiasm and commitment that made Doublet a champion event horse and Windsor Bob an unbeatable gun dog. Other heads of state may own large country estates, but none are as readily identified with them as the British royal family are with their country homes at Windsor, Sandringham, Balmoral and, more recently, Gatcombe.

Left *The Queen travels to Windsor, guarded by the household cavalry*

Below left *The Glass Coach has been used for many royal weddings. Here the carriage horses are proudly displayed with their trophies*

ROYAL ANIMALS OF STATE AND CEREMONY

*T*he magnificent chargers on which Her Majesty rides to review the Trooping of the Colour each year are as much symbols of her sovereignty as the more orthodox crown and sceptre. Even though the importance of the horse in the national economy has greatly reduced since the reign of Queen Elizabeth I, Queen Elizabeth II still appears on horseback on the obverse of her Great Seal of the Realm, just as her forebear and namesake did four hundred years ago.

When Duke William of Normandy came ashore at Pevensey in 1066 he brought with him more than Noman French and continental cuisine. He brought the large Normandy horses from whom all the great chargers of medieval battles took their line. The native Celtic ponies were no match for these Norman steeds and it was probably Duke William's cavalry superiority that secured his new kingdom for him.

Throughout the Middle Ages succeeding kings took steps to improve the quality and stature of English battle-horses. At the turn of the thirteenth century King John imported more than one hundred black Flemish stallions that were probably the ancestors of the mighty shire horses.

The great success of English armies in the following century must have been due in part to the quality of the horses on which the knights rode into battle at celebrated victories like Crécy and Poitiers. Although ironically Edward III, the victor at these two decisive battles, reviewed his troops at Crécy mounted on a small, gentle palfrey.

Thirty-two years before, however, he had suffered a disastrous defeat at the hands of the Scots at Bannockburn, which resulted in the wholesale slaughter of the nation's finest horses. So for several years afterwards horses were hard to come by in England and their export was strictly forbidden, especially north of the border. In fact laws to curb the sale of English horses abroad existed from Edward's reign until the time of Henry VIII.

The developments in medieval warfare had resulted in the need for mounted knights to carry far heavier armour in Henry's reign than they had in Edward III's. Since the horses were clad in their own armour as well, they were expected to carry a total weight amounting to a fifth of a ton. Clearly any animal capable of bearing this could not be agile as well as strong, and the great ponderous battle horses of the Tudors were gradually relegated to the fields and farmyards where a few of their successors can still be seen.

The subjects of Queen Elizabeth I could hardly have failed to associate proud, upstanding horses with their Queen who spent so much of her time in magnificent mounted progresses around her realm. On the stage, too, the intimate connection between the sovereign and his horse had not escaped William Shakespeare. His Richard III is left standing in the middle of Bosworth Field crying:

> ' A horse! A horse! My kingdom
> for a horse.'

While less than forty lines before his death Richard II discovers that his rival and usurper, Henry Bolingbroke, rode to his Coronation, as Henry IV, on Richard's own favourite horse, Roan Barbary.

Charles I was the outstanding Stuart horseman whose love of fine horses and the rapidly developing skill of dressage can be seen in the

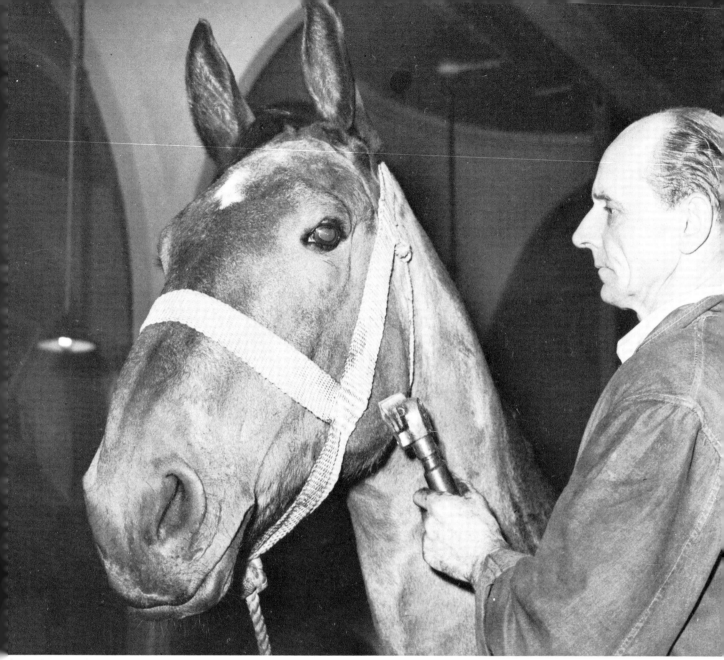

magnificent portraits of him on horseback painted by Van Dyck. But it is to the Hanoverian monarchs that we really owe the tradition of horses of state and ceremony that has lasted until this day.

The White Horse was the heraldic badge of the house of Hanover and throughout his reign George I imported horses from his native Germany to be used at state occasions in his new kingdom. The celebrated cream stallions which he introduced were used on state occasions until 1920. They were bred at the Royal Stud, then situated at Hampton Court, and were only supplanted by the blacks, bays and greys, when replacements became impossible to find in the twentieth century.

George III bought what was to become Buckingham Palace in 1762, but it was left to his son, George IV to construct the Royal Mews that we know today. The responsibilities of the Crown Equerry at the Royal Mews have broadened in the twentieth century to include the royal limousines and other family cars, as well as the organisation of all road travel and royal processions. However, horses and state carriages still form a major part of his concerns.

In 1947 King George VI asked his Crown Equerry to find a horse that would be suitable for his elder daughter to ride at the Trooping of the Colour that year, and to ensure that Princess Elizabeth was taught how to ride in this form of display. The horse that the equerry found was Tommy and the instructor was Mrs. Archer Houblon.

Although a horsewoman of considerable skill and experience, the Princess began to learn how to ride side-saddle with her characteristic conscientiousness and attention to detail. In the indoor riding school at Buckingham Palace Mrs. Archer Houblon taught her how to sit correctly both at the walk and at all other paces.

Tommy for his part proved an equally responsive pupil. After the tranquil meadows of the Duke of Beaufort's home at Badminton the noise and bustle of London must have been a frightening change. However, he was ridden through the traffic-filled streets and taken to railway stations and playgrounds to get used to the noises of large crowds, and he quickly adapted to his new role.

The Princess's participation in the birthday parade was a closely guarded secret and the press and the public only got wind of what was afoot when Mrs. Archer Houblon appeared riding Tommy side-saddle at the dress rehearsals for the ceremony.

The twenty-one year old Princess was a striking figure when she rode to Horse Guards Parade on that June morning. Wearing a simple navy-blue uniform she was following the pattern set by Queen Victoria, who in the first year of her reign inspected the 1st Regiment of the Life Guards, the Grenadier Guards and a squadron of lancers, mounted on a charger named Leopold. The sight of the young Queen on horseback, inspecting her troops, in her own words 'like a man', made a profound impression on soldiers and spectators alike. And when Lord Melbourne, her Prime Minister, advised her the following year to inspect the military review in Hyde Park from a carriage, both the Queen and her subjects were greatly disappointed.

In 1948 Princess Elizabeth rode her father's chestnut police horse, Winston, at the Trooping of the Colour, when the King was too ill to ride himself and had to be content with riding in a carriage.

Winston remained Her Majesty's mount for nine years. A large horse, measuring over sixteen hands, he behaved impeccably whenever he was on parade, and only on two occasions did he fidget and move during the march past. Both of these lapses were due to irritating discomforts; the first was from flies and on the second occasion a rucked saddle cloth was the culprit.

Winston's successor was another police horse called Imperial. He joined the Metropolitan police as a three-year-old and though of a more lively, and sometimes obstreperous nature, he quickly showed that he could behave well in crowds and would be well suited to being ridden side-saddle. Imperial became a firm favourite with his handlers and

Right The red morocco harness is used for coronations
Above left Individual carriage horses are less well known, but in the 1950's Rudolph was a great favourite. Faultless in obedience and pulling power, he could be used in any position

with the general public. In his stables at Great Scotland Yard he was brought breakfast, an apple and a cup of tea, in bed every morning. While in the public parades and shows that he attended there were no end of goodies willingly offered to satisfy his sweet tooth.

In later years Her Majesty has ridden her well-known Canadian ceremonial horses Burmese and Centennial, presented to her by the Mounties, but these share the characteristics of their predecessors. They are and look every inch chargers, and it is a testamony of the Queen's riding skill that she always looks so composed and completely at ease mounted on these massive animals and surrounded by thousands of cheering sightseers.

Fortunately no accident has ever occurred during the Trooping of the Colour, probably as a result of the great care taken in schooling the horses. However, Her Majesty's grandfather broke his pelvis in two places after an accident in similar circumstances during the Great War. King George usually inspected his troops on foot, but on this occasion it was suggested that he would be seen better if he was on horseback. However, just as he was leaving an impromptu cheer from the men startled the horse which slipped in the mud and fell back on the King, bruising him terribly and giving him an awful shock.

Trooping the Colour is the only occasion when the Queen rides side-saddle and the only

time too when she appears in public on horseback. Conscious of the importance of the occasion and always meticulous in her preparation, Her Majesty will spend a month beforehand practising in the riding school at Buckingham Palace. She has to re-accustom her leg muscles to the demands of riding sidesaddle, as well as practising the control of her mount using only one hand on the reins: the other hand has to be kept free for saluting.

Nearer the day itself, Prince Philip, Prince Charles and the other members of the royal family involved in the ceremony will familiarise themselves with their own mounts. For many years Prince Philip rode Linnhe, a brown mare from Rochester Row police station. The horses, too, have to get used to the frightening spectacle of a bearskin and the flashing arms and armour of the Household Cavalry.

On the morning of the birthday parade the horses are harnessed with their ceremonial bridles, with silk rosettes on the browband in red or blue, and the military saddles and saddle cloths which they wear. The Queen's horse is saddled with a gold-embroidered blue saddle cloth and a magnificent side-saddle with one gold-gilt stirrup. The barouches that will carry other members of the royal family are drawn into the Inner Quadrangle of the palace to collect their passengers. As soon as they have departed, the Queen and the other

royal riders emerge from the King's Door and mount their horses held waiting for them by footmen, attended by the Crown Equerry and the Master of the Horse. The finishing touches are made to Her Majesty's habit, the last polish is given to the horses' bridles and the royal party ride under the archway to be greeted by a tumultuous roar from the waiting crowds. For the horses this is the climax of their weeks of preparation, for once they have returned to the palace at the head of the marching soldiers, their royal riders dismount, thank them for their services and they are then led away to return to their normal duties, on the beat. Only the special ceremonial horses like Burmese and Centennial return to the Royal Stables at Windsor.

Of course there are many horses kept at the Royal Mews and these are the ones used as carriage horses. The famous cream horses introduced by George I were used on occasions of highest state for over two hundred years. In the 1920's these were replaced by black horses, also of Hanoverian origin, which in turn were replaced after a couple of years' service by the bays.

The bays in the Royal Mews today are still largely Cleveland bays, the only British-bred carriage horses. These have been developed

Above left The Queen is mounted on Burmese for the 1970 Trooping of the Colour

Above The drummers of the Household Cavalry ride piebald or skewbald horses

Below Princess Margaret and the Queen Mother ride together with Prince Charles and Princess Anne in one of the open state landaus

from the original Cleveland bays which were sturdy, little animals that resembled pack ponies. Crossed with the thoroughbred they produced the Yorkshire coach horse which became a popular carriage horse during the early years of this century.

The famous Windsor greys sound as if they are a special breed, whereas in fact they owe their name to the royal residence where they were first used for drawing the private carriages of the royal family. Grey horses had been kept at Windsor from before Queen Victoria's reign, but it was only after the reign of King George V that they were transferred to the Royal Mews at Buckingham Palace. Today the Windsor greys mainly come from the West German Oldenburg breed, although there are one or two English and Irish greys amongst them.

Some of the carriage horses are named after specific royal events. The greys Santiago and Rio were named after state visits made by the Queen to Chile and Brazil. Others like the Cleveland bays Lady Penelope and Batman have no such claim to auspicious royal events. However, the carriage horses are seldom as easily distinguished as the individual royal mounts — as far as the public are concerned they appear in teams of two or more to draw the royal carriages in the traditional parades and celebrations that form so much of our royal pageantry.

The horses and their immaculately liveried postillions are complemented by the collection of elegant royal carriages in the Royal Mews, of which the Gold State Coach takes pride of place. This splendid royal coach was commissioned at the beginning of the reign of George III. When it was finally delivered to the Royal Mews early in the morning of 24 November 1762, it was the most expensive coach ever built in the kingdom. The journal kept by the Clerk of the Stables, which is still in the Royal Mews, records that the coach was indeed 'very superb'. It was gilded all over and beautifully decorated with panels painted by Giovanni Cipriani. Twenty-four feet long, twelve feet high, over eight feet wide and weighing four tons, the coach needed to be drawn by eight horses. Following its trial run in the Royal

Mews that winter morning over two hundred years ago the new coach was found to be satisfactory and the following day the King rode in it drawn by eight of his Hanoverian creams to open the session of Parliament. The Gold State Coach has been a success ever since and it has been used in the coronation of every sovereign from George IV to that of Her Majesty the Queen in 1953.

In the year of the Queen's Silver Jubilee, 1977, the coach was completely refurbished, for probably the first time in its existence. It was regilded by the experienced firm, Cambell, Smith and Company and the crimson satin upholstery was repaired with specially woven matching material.

Right *The Royal Mews was originally in Charing Cross, on the present site of the National Gallery*

Below *The Queen Mother distributes the traditional shamrock to the Irish Guards. Even their mascot, the Irish wolfhound Cormac of Tara, is not forgotten*

Although it has always been drawn by eight horses, the Gold State Coach, unlike all the others, can only be driven at walking pace, which is probably just as well for the walking grooms, footmen, beefeaters and brakeman who accompany the coach in its ceremonial progress.

The team of eight horses is harnessed in pairs with four of them being ridden by postillions; although originally the first six horses were driven by a coachman, with only the leading pair being postillion-ridden. However, King Edward VII who felt that the driving box and driver prevented people from seeing the occupants of the coach, had the box removed, which necessitated having four postillions instead of the original one.

The Irish State Coach is traditionally used by the Queen when she attends the State Opening of Parliament and it was in this coach that she returned to Buckingham Palace after watching the Silver Jubilee Firework Display.

The Scottish State Coach is the lightest and brightest of all the royal coaches. It is used by the Queen on state visits to Scotland and it was a Scottish organisation, the St. Cuthbert's Co-operative Society, which made a completely new top for this coach in 1969, giving it large glass windows and two glass lights in the roof, which give overhead spectators as good a view of the coach's occupants as those standing at ground level.

Another coach with large windows is the Glass Coach, as its name implies. This is the coach used at most royal weddings. Both the Queen and Prince Philip, and Princess Anne and Captain Mark Phillips were driven from Westminster Abbey to Buckingham Palace in this after their respective weddings.

Some of the most attractive royal carriages are the open landaus which are always popular with the crowds lining the routes of royal processions because they afford uninterrupted views of their passengers. Of these the most important is the 1902 State Landau which is usually drawn by six of the Windsor greys. The Queen uses this landau to meet visiting heads of state when they arrive on official visits, and it was in this that she and

Prince Philip returned to Buckingham Palace from the Guildhall during the Silver Jubilee celebrations.

The lighter state landaus provide transport for members of the royal family and other dignitaries on state occasions. These are generally drawn by a pair of bays and were formerly driven with the roof closed as the footmen riding behind had some difficulty in staying on the carriage when the roof was down. However, in recent years detachable seats have been added, which has made the conversion of these to open carriages rather more practical, and considerably more comfortable for the footmen.

Royal carriages have always been closely associated with racing at Ascot. One of the high points of the annual Royal Ascot meeting is the royal carriage procession up the course. This is in fact one of the earliest royal processions, and it dates from the reign of that other great royal horsewoman, Queen Anne, who commanded that a racecourse should be laid out on Ascot Heath. On 11 August, 1711, she inaugurated the first race meeting there with a carriage procession from Windsor to Ascot.

George IV, another royal devotee of the Turf, instituted the actual procession up the course, though he was accompanied by the Windsor buckhounds. Some sixty years later the Prince of Wales made a similar procession though, in addition to the royal buckhounds, he was attended by the royal whippers-in, and the royal park keepers as well as the usual footmen and postillions.

The hunting entourage was disbanded when he came to the throne as Edward VII, but the original procession has continued in the basketwork-sided carriages still used today. Traditionally the first carriage has been drawn by four grey horses, preceded by two outriders mounted on grey horses, while the others have each been drawn by four bays, preceded by a single outrider mounted on a further bay.

One curious fact about the colours of all the royal carriage horses is that chestnut horses never seem to have been popular at the Royal Mews. In all the records stretching back to the reign of George II, there is no mention of a chestnut having ever been employed as a harness horse.

In addition to the horses used by the royal family on state occasions, the other horses that catch the attention of the sightseers are those of the Household Cavalry. This is formed by three of the oldest and most prestigious regiments in the English Army that date back to the time of the Civil War; though since 1969, two of these regiments have been amalgamated to form the Blues and Royals.

The ceremonial uniform worn by both regiments is essentially the same, except that the Life Guards wear a red tunic, whereas the Blues and Royals, as their name suggests, wear a blue tunic. In each regiment the Farrier carries a highly polished axe on important ceremonial occasions, a symbol of his trade, and a tool which his predecessors once used. In both the regiments Farriers wear blue tunics, but the Farrier in the Life Guards has a black plume to his helmet.

The horses of both regiments are the same as well. All the horses are black except for those of the trumpeters which are grey and those ridden by the drummers, which are either piebald or skewbald.

Above *In this painting by Leonard Boden, the Queen is mounted on Imperial*

Opposite page *The coaches wait outside Westminster while a royal wedding is in progress*

Throughout its history the Household Cavalry has been closely associated with the royal family. The first Life Guards assembled round the fugitive Prince Charles when he was exiled during the Commonwealth period and, since the Restoration, the regular duties of the Household Cavalry have been to mount the guard at royal residences and provide the Sovereign's Escort.

Of all the animals connected with state and ceremony, though, none enjoys a more unique position than an Irish wolfhound named Cormac of Tara. He is the mascot of the Irish Guards and the only regimental mascot in the whole of the Household Division. Irish wolfhounds have led the Irish Guards on ceremonial occasions since 1902, and Cormac is the seventh of that distinguished line.

Above, near right, below and below right *In 1939 Princess Elizabeth and Princess Margaret made a surprise visit to the London Zoo. We can catch a glimpse of that afternoon in this charming series of photographs*

Far right *There are other connections with more exotic animals. In 1956 the Russian leaders Bulganin and Kruschev presented Princess Anne with a bear cub, Nikki. It first appeared in public at the London Zoo with another home-bred cub, Rusk*

Left *Prince Charles too may have been tempted by one of the famous Barbary Apes. Here they make friends during a visit to Gibraltar in 1954*

THE ROYAL ZOO OF HERALDRY

*T*o most of us the mention of royal heraldic beasts brings to mind two animals, the lion and the unicorn. These are the ones which appear on either side of the royal coat of arms. However, there are many more beasts in the royal heraldic zoo which we see every day of our lives without giving them a second glance.

Probably the greatest number of pub signs have originated from coats of arms and heraldic badges, and of these the majority are connected with the badges of the kings and queens in our history.

Even so, how many of us popping into the *White Hart* give a thought to Richard II? How many in the *Black Lion* think of Anne of Cleves, the fourth wife of Henry VIII, or of Philippa, the wife of Edward III, who begged for the lives of the burgesses of Calais? In the *Greyhound* or the *Falcon* Edward VI never crosses our mind, and in the *Red Lion,* the most common pub sign in England, we think little of John of Gaunt who was the most powerful man in the kingdom for thirty years. Yet they all bore these animals on their badges, and the chances are that the pubs were named after them, or their families.

These royal beasts were probably first used as a means of easy identification in the heat of medieval battles, when one knight in armour looked much the same as the next and when the only rallying points on the confused field of battle were the standards of either side. It was not long, though, before they became popular as decorations. Henry VIII seems to have been particularly fond of them. He decorated the medieval bridge at Rochester with ten royal beasts in 1536. He liberally scattered them around Hampton Court after Cardinal Wolsey had given the palace to him, and ten of his royal beasts can still be seen on the lintel of the magnificent fireplace in the Castle Library at Windsor.

Elizabeth I was as keen on royal beasts as her father. In 1588, the year of the Spanish Armada, she ordered four of them, a lion, a dragon, a greyhound and a bull, to be placed on the landing stage at Greenwich. And three hundred and sixty-five years later, these four appeared with six others at the entrance to Westminster Abbey when our own Queen was crowned Elizabeth II on 2nd June 1953.

The ten beasts chosen for the Coronation were those that most closely reflected the Queen's royal descent. These and many others have been used by kings and queens throughout our history. The ones chosen here are among the most well known.

The Lion

The lion was regarded as the king of animals for centuries before heraldry was even thought of, and it seems likely that chieftains used it as a symbol of their power and office in many ancient cultures. In Britain the twelfth century historian Geoffrey of Monmouth recorded in his *Prophecies of Merlin,* the legendary wizard of King Arthur, that the Lion of Justice would restore order to the troubled land. Both William the Conqueror and his son William Rufus used lions on their royal seals, but no lion appears on a royal coat of arms until the reign of Henry I. He used a single lion on his badge, and many believe that this is the Lion of Justice referred to in the *Prophecies of Merlin*, especially as under Henry I the country saw the establishment of an effective administrative and legal system for the first time since the Conquest. It

is interesting, too, that the first lion ever seen in England arrived during his reign and was kept at the royal residence at Woodstock.

It was Henry's great-grandson, Richard I, or Richard the Lionheart, who first established the pattern of using three golden lions, one above another and set on a red background, as the Royal Arms of England. These appeared on a seal cut in 1195 and, since then, they have been adopted by every king or queen who has ascended the throne of England.

The Lion of England was used on other royal decorations as well. Henry III had a lion set on the gable-end of his hall at Windsor and he even added four little lions to his great seal, two rearing at the sides of the throne and two acting as a foot-stool. In the reign of Edward III, lions and lion-heads appeared on the ensigns flown on the King's ships. However, it is only comparatively recently, since the accession of James I in 1603, that the crowned lion has been fixed as the supporter (beast on one side of the shield) to the royal arms, together with the unicorn of Scotland.

Up until that time sovereigns frequently changed their supporters during their reigns, and there was no certainty of continuity from one reign to the next.

The White Lion

The White Lion has been inherited by the Queen from Edward IV, who in turn inherited it from his grandmother's family, the Mortimers. Consequently, it is referred to as the White Lion of Mortimer. Unlike the Lion of England, the White Lion of Mortimer has no crown, and whereas the English lion is usually shown standing on one leg, or 'rampant' in heraldic terminology, the lion of the Mortimers usually sits when it appears on a shield.

Edward IV and the House of York used the Mortimer lion on many of their arms. Edward used it as a supporter to the Royal Arms, either in conjunction with one of his other beasts or on its own, with a lion on either side. This connection with the House of York has lasted ever since, and when the White Lion of Mortimer was displayed at the Coronation in 1953, it held a shield on which was mounted a white rose surrounded by a circle of golden rays. This was the badge that had been used by the Queen's father, King George VI, when he was Duke of York.

The badge is itself the combination of two distinct badges used by the House of York, the white rose, made famous in the Wars of the Roses and the sun badge which, according to legend, was adopted by Edward IV as a commemoration of the appearance of three suns the day before his famous victory at the battle of Mortimer's Cross. In Edward's eyes, this strange phenomenon was an omen of his victory and when this was proved to be correct, he adopted the sun as one of his heraldic badges. He also used it frequently with the white rose of York.

The Greyhound

The greyhound is one of the oldest and most prestigious dogs man has ever bred. The Pharaohs of Fourth Dynasty Egypt depicted greyhounds on the walls of their tombs; greyhounds appear on ancient carvings in Africa and Asia and, in Europe, greyhounds were associated with the aristocracy from the Dark Ages until the nineteenth century.

A law passed during the reign of King Canute stated that: 'No meane person may keep any greyhounds.' The law itself labours the point which would have been all too obvious to the King's subjects, to whom the ownership of a greyhound was literally as unlikely as employing servants. At that time the price of a greyhound was the same as that of a serf!

Before the Magna Carta the law decreed that the destruction of a greyhound should carry the same capital penalty as the murder of a man, and King John was prepared on more than one occasion to accept two or three greyhounds from his subjects in lieu of tax.

As an heraldic beast, the greyhound was evidently as popular as other beasts associated with that most virile of medieval pursuits, hunting, or the chase. Greyhounds were certainly used on the arms of the Royal House before Henry Tudor defeated Richard III at Bosworth Field in 1485. However, the victorious Henry VII was so partial to the greyhound that its introduction into the roy-

al heraldic zoo is frequently credited to him.

Henry VII's greyhound was white and it wore a red collar edged and studded with gold and with a gold ring. It appeared on the King's standards, in St. George's Chapel at Windsor hanging above the Royal Pew, on the bridge at Rochester and later on the bridge at Hampton Court. In fact, wherever the royal beasts congregated, the white greyhound was sure to be among them.

Henry VII inherited the white greyhound from his father, Edmund, who had been created Earl of Richmond in 1453, and the beast itself is referred to in this context as the White Greyhound of Richmond. The beast had descended to him as well from John of Gaunt, through Henry's mother, Lady Margaret Beaufort, and if these family ties were

Opposite page *The first lion ever seen in England belonged to Henry I and was kept in the royal menagerie at Woodstock*
Below *Richard the Lionheart first used the three golden lions set against a red background for the royal arms of England*

Henry VII.

Richard III.

in need of additional support, Henry's use of the greyhound has close associations with another Henry who used it, Henry IV.

Henry IV was the son of John of Gaunt and, like his father, wore the greyhound as his badge, which gave him the nickname of 'the Dog.' The nickname was further merited in view of the fact that the future Henry IV literally hounded the White Hart, Richard II, defeated him and drove his dispirited followers from the Kingdom.

Henry VII must have seen close similarities between his own defeat of the White Boar, Richard III, and his namesake's defeat of Richard II eighty-five years before. And this must have lent added enthusiasm to his adoption of the White Greyhound.

This enthusiasm did not end with Henry VII. The greyhound was a popular beast throughout the Tudor dynasty and beyond. As late as the end of the eighteenth century, King's Messengers were still wearing silver greyhound badges on their sleeves as a token of their office.

The Horse

In the terms of British royal heraldry, the most common horse is the White Horse. This breed has an interesting pedigree, originating in Westphalia, in Germany, but leading to the appearance of two separate horses from the same stud divided by over one thousand years.

The White Horse has appeared on the arms of the County of Kent for centuries. It appears on the caps and blazer badges of Kent County Cricket Club as well as on the arms of Margate, Ramsgate, Dartford and Strood; not to mention the London boroughs of Bexley and Lewisham that formerly fell within the county boundaries.

Tradition holds that the White Horse appeared with the Saxon invaders Hengist and Horsa. To a certain extent this is true. The White Horse was evidently a pre-heraldic Saxon device used by these chieftains who claimed their descent from the Norse god Odin, the owner of a fabulous horse called Sleipner.

Hengist and Horsa, however, were figures of legend, though not without interest in the horse's pedigree. The Frisians called 'a horse' 'hengist', and the Anglians called it 'horsa'. So it seems likely that whoever led the invading forces fifteen centuries ago, the White Horse was his emblem, and as such it was afterwards adopted by the kings of Kent.

As with many beasts that eventually found their way onto royal heraldic shields and badges, the white horse served a utilitarian as well as symbolic purpose. Proud, virile and fierce as it was, it also fulfilled an important religious function. Its neighing presaged the outcome of battles, presumably through the agency of the god Odin.

Odin was long forgotten when the horse made its second appearance on the royal arms, but the horse galloping across the shield was essentially the same. This was the White Horse of Hanover, introduced into the Royal Arms following the death of Queen Anne in 1714. It was borne by a grandson of Princess Elizabeth, the sister of Charles I. His name was Elector George of Hanover, who on his accession to the throne styled himself George I, King of Great Britain, France and Ireland, Duke of Brunswick-Luneburg.

The arms of Hanover, on which the horse appeared, were removed from the Royal Arms in 1837, when Queen Victoria ascended the throne. As a woman she was barred from inheriting the throne of Hanover and the title and arms passed to her eldest son, the Duke of Cumberland. However, the White Horse of Hanover was still borne by the badges of several regiments like the West Yorkshire Regiment, the King's (Liverpool) Regiment and the 3rd King's Own Hussars in later years.

In more recent times it has made an appropriate reappearance on the arms of Princess Anne's husband, Captain Mark Phillips.

The White Hart

Medieval hunters showed great respect for the wild animals they chased as well as for the animals they used in the hunt. The deer was probably the noblest of these, providing as it did both excellent sport and a source of food for the royal table.

In royal heraldry the White Hart has become virtually synonymous with Richard II, whose great popularity led to the proliferation of pubs and inns bearing his noble beast on their signs.

Richard's White Hart appears collared with his crown, in heraldic terms 'gorged' and this crown-collar carries a chain. This is in fact an ancient symbol that has its roots in a legend claiming that the original White Hart was captured and collared by Alexander the Great. Alexander was a popular figure in medieval folklore, and any association with him would have been an advantage to the King.

In addition to its frequent appearance on pub signs up and down the country, Richard's White Hart is also prominent on the arms of Derby, which show a hart sitting in a ring fence on a green shield. And following his expedition to Ireland in 1394, the present crest of Ireland was adopted, showing a white hart springing from a triple-turreted tower.

There are several explanations for Richard's adoption of this clearly attractive beast. His mother bore a White Hind as her heraldic badge, and there may have been a visual pun intended by the King whose Christian name can be divided into Rich-hart. Whatever the reason for its adoption, it has become one of the most durable and popular royal beasts of England.

The White Boar

Just as popular belief has often associated the White Hart with good King Richard II, so it has connected the ferocious, evil-looking boar with his namesake, the greatly maligned Richard III.

It is by no means clear why he adopted it. Three popular theories exist, though they are all of doubtful foundation.

83

YALE OF BEAUFORT

The first assumes a visual pun between the boar and 'Ebor' the abbreviated form of the Roman name for York 'Eboracum'. Richard was Duke of Gloucester, however, and though of the House of York, he never held the title himself. What is more, those who did hold the honour never used the boar as a badge.

Another pun theory suggests that the title 'Rex Angliae', King of England, might have been punned with the heraldic term for a boar 'sanglier'. The fact that Richard used the boar as his badge before he became king makes this doubtful, too.

Lastly a theory doubtless put about by Richard's enemies implies a sense of ironic, defiant, cynicism on his part. If he was indeed hunchbacked and repulsive, the boar would have made an appropriate symbol of these deformities. However, it is by no means certain that his appearance, or his manner, were as evil as his legend has suggested.

The boar was a worthy adversary to the medieval hunter, ranking with the deer. As a fierce beast it was well qualified as a heraldic badge and this seems the likeliest explanation of its use by Richard III.

His reign was not without its blemishes, even if he was not wholly responsible for the murder of the princes in the Tower. Arthur Collingbourne of Wiltshire was executed after writing this popular jingle:

'The Cat, the Rat, and Lovell our Dog
Rule all England under an Hog.'

The four beasts refer to the badges of the King, Sir William Catesby, Sir Richard Ratcliffe and Lord Lovell. And it is reported that following Richard's defeat at Bosworth Field, many inns bearing his White Boar had their beasts painted blue overnight. The blue boar was the sign of the Earl of Oxford who was one of the staunchest supporters of Henry Tudor. In those days it paid to be seen on the right side in any civil war.

The Black Bull

The Black Bull of Clarence has passed to the Queen down the same line as the White Lion of Mortimer, through her ancestor, Edward IV. He claimed the Black Bull from Lionel, the Duke of Clarence, whose grandson Roger had been nominated by Richard II as his successor. Roger's claim to the throne was usurped by Henry IV, and he was eventually murdered in Ireland. As his great-grandson, Edward IV asserted, the intervening Lancastrian kings, Henry IV, Henry V and Henry VI, had merely interrupted his true line of descent from Roger Mortimer, and on that basis he

The Queen's Beasts stand majestically in front of the palm house at Kew Gardens. These three are the Yale of Beaufort, the Unicorn of Scotland and the Red Dragon of Wales

RED DRAGON O

justified his defeat and overthrow of Henry VI in 1461.

The Black Bull of Clarence appears on the arms of Clare College, Cambridge, which was founded by Elizabeth de Clare, from whom the bull eventually passed to Lionel, Duke of Clarence, who used it on his seal. It was also used by Edward IV from time to time and occasionally by Richard III.

It was placed among the Yorkist beasts on the roof of St. George's Chapel, Windsor, where it can still be seen. It is also one of the beasts on the bridge at Hampton Court, and there it can be seen holding a Tudor rose.

The Falcon

The royal falcon is principally associated with Edward III who adopted the bird after his passion for the princely sport. He gave the name of 'Falcon' to one of his Knights of Arms and the bird passed to his younger sons John of Gaunt and Edmund of Langley from whom sprang the great rivals of the Wars of the Roses, with the result that the falcon appears on the badges of participants in both sides of the contest.

In many cases the falcon appears with a fetterlock, which looks like a padlock to us. This was used on the badge of John of Gaunt and Edmund of Langley where it appears closed, which may have implied that as the king's younger sons, they had no hope of becoming kings themselves. Likewise the fetterlock on the badge of Edward IV's son, Richard Duke of York appears open, which could be taken to indicate that Edward had 'forced the lock' in order to obtain the crown. The badge

that the Queen has inherited has appeared with the fetterlock open ever since the reign of Edward IV.

Queen Elizabeth I also made considerable use of the falcon. She had inherited it from her mother Anne Boleyn, who had been given it by Henry VIII at their wedding. The falcon served a dual purpose in this marriage gift. As a royal badge it symbolised the new Queen's elevation to the royal family, but it also represented the Queen herself, for her father Sir Thomas Boleyn had been awarded the earldom of Ormande by the King, and this title carried with it the badge of the falcon as well.

The Eagle

The eagle probably made its first symbolic appearance in Britain at the time of the Roman invasion. Since then it has been amalgamated into Celtic folklore and has appeared in royal heraldry since the thirteenth century.

The first English king to be credited with the use of the eagle was Henry II who according to the sixteenth century historian William Camden had it painted in his bedchamber at Windsor. He goes on to tell us that four young chickens were painted with the eagle:

'wherwof three pecked and scratched him, the fourth picked out his eyes'.

As Camden explains, this represented the King's four sons who contrived his downfall, the last being John, Henry's youngest son of whom he was most fond, yet who was cruellest to his father.

In the Celtic connection the eagle appears on the first seal of Caernarvon where it is positioned above the Lions of England. The eagle had been associated with Owen Gwynedd, one of the kings of North Wales who had died in 1169. In 1371 an eagle was set on the large tower of Caernarvon Castle which later became known as the Eagle Tower. Furthermore the reigning monarch at that time was Edward III, who was sometimes referred to as the 'Eagle'.

One later royal association is that of the Duchy of Lancaster. Henry V, Henry VI, Henry VII and Henry VIII all depicted the eagle on the signets they used for their affairs connected with the Duchy.

The Swan

The swan was a popular bird during the middle ages. Its beauty and stately grace endeared it to many noble families that adopted the bird as their badge. It had a noble and ancient affiliation with the legendary Swan Knight, Lohengrin, from whom many great families claimed descent and it was regarded by many as an emblem of regal poise, grace and innocence.

The swan entered the menagerie of royal beasts from the de Bohun family, when Mary de Bohun married Henry of Lancaster in 1380. The swan then became a Lancastrian badge and was used particularly by the Princes of Wales in the fifteenth century. It was a badge favoured by both Henry IV and his son Henry V, the victor of Agincourt.

The swan was regarded as a bird royal for other reasons too. Apart from its apparent grace and gentleness, it had several practical uses. Kings and warriors would swear oaths on the swan. The swan was also a principal dish in great feasts, both of the aristocracy and the great City companies. The Brewer's Company in particular were famous for the swans served at their feasts and in the records of the Northumberland family the household accounts show 'XX swanes' consumed between Christmas Day and Twelfth Night in one year.

The swan is still a bird royal of course and the Queen shares the swans on the Thames with the Vinters' and Dyers' Companies.

The Unicorn

The spread of travel knowledge generated by the crusades and the journeys of merchants and pilgrims to the Mediterranean and North Africa gave rise to scraps of bizarre information which ultimately produced some amazing heraldic beasts. The account of one encounter with a giraffe, which the traveller in question took to be the hybrid offspring of camel and a leopard led to the creation of the 'camelopard' by which the giraffe is still named in heraldic terminology.

In the royal heraldic zoo the foremost of these fabulous beasts is the unicorn, the emblem of Scotland. In appearance the unicorn

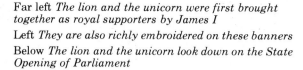
is an amalgam of many of the noblest of heraldic beasts. To the head, body and mane of a horse, are added the tail of a lion, the limbs and hoofs of a stag, the tufted beard of a goat and the single, straight horn with its spiral twist to which the beast owes its name.

The earliest description of a unicorn, dating from about 400 B.C. seems to describe the animal as a curious combination of a rhinoceros, a desert antelope and a giant bull. The beast was remarkable for its prodigious strength and its great and haughty mind; as one authority wrote by way of explanation: 'he is never caught alive; kylled he may be but taken he cannot be.'

The practice adopted by Bible translators of using the word 'unicorn' whenever they failed to translate an obscure Hebrew name, confirmed the beast's existence in the minds of the faithful. Even sailors began to accept the horn of the Narwhal as that of the unicorn, although the unicorn was clearly a terrestrial animal. Although no one had ever seen a unicorn, the animal certainly existed in the fauna of the Middle Ages.

During the course of its lengthy history the unicorn underwent significant changes. It became gradually reduced in size from the beast that was so large that it could not fit into the ark and had to be towed behind, to the size of a young goat. Its fierce sense of independence remained, though a means of catching it was discovered, the manifestly erotic use of a beautiful, young virgin. Left alone by the hunters the girl was believed to attract the unicorn, which promptly laid its head in her lap and went to sleep, allowing the hunters to stealthily return and capture or kill the beast. Somehow this was contrived to form an allegory of Christ's Incarnation and Passion and the unicorn far from being a symbol of lust or male potency, became a symbol of chastity and innocence.

This was matched by a similar belief in the power of the unicorn's horn as a water-conner for the beasts. Somewhere in its confused pedigree, the unicorn had been endowed with the power of determining the presence of, and acting as an antidote to, any poison. To medieval man the unicorn's horn was equally beneficial. Apothecaries frequently displayed it outside their shops and fragments of unicorn horn exchanged hands at exorbitant prices. Queen Elizabeth I kept a piece of unicorn horn at Windsor, which even in those days was valued at £10,000. And the scholarly James I even presented his wife with 'one little cup of unicorn horn' which had belonged to Queen Bess.

It was through James that the unicorn entered the royal arms of England. It had been a Scottish royal beast for nearly two hundred years and James III of Scotland had struck coins bearing unicorns during his reign. But when James I ascended the English throne in 1603 the royal supporters, the lion and the unicorn, became firmly established and have remained unchanged on the Royal Arms to this day.

This was not the first time that the two beasts had been juxtaposed. As far back as the heyday of ancient Rome an Egyptian artist had drawn a unicorn and a lion playing a game of draughts, which the lion appears to have won.

Edmund Spenser, the Elizabethan author of *The Fairie Queen* had referred to the unhappy co-existence of the two beasts which reflected the animosity between England and Scotland in the lines:

'Like as a lyon whose imperiall powre
A proud rebellious unicorne defyes.'

However, the union of the two countries was confirmed one hundred years after James I became King of England and the lion and the unicorn have kept their mutual distrust and fierce independence under strict control ever since.

The Dragon

Dragons have been revered, feared, worshipped and despised from China to Cornwall. The dragon of the Far East has always been a benign creature, but in the West it has been regarded as the most evil and frightening beast on Earth. In Christian symbolism the dragon was equated with the devil.

In Britain the dragon has long be associated with the Celts. It was the symbol of the Welsh chieftain Cadwallader two centuries after the Romans left Britain, and he had probably adopted it from the Roman symbol of the cohort, which had served as a military ensign during the period of their occupation. The Celtic word 'dragon' meant 'a chief' and Cadwallader's own name translated meant 'Red Dragon Dreadful'.

According to legend Uther, the father of King Arthur, took the dragon as his symbol, after seeing a pair of dragons flying in the sky. He took their appearance as a sign that he would be King and consequently had two dragons made. One he gave to Winchester, and the other he carried as his standard into battle. His second name, Pendragon, means 'Chief Dragon'.

Later, and on firmer historical ground, the West Saxons, who landed near Southampton in 495 adopted the golden dragon as their standard. King Harold raised a golden dragon at Hastings and this is recorded twice in the Bayeux tapestry. Even after the Norman conquest the dragon was still revered, so clearly whatever stigma may have been attached to the dragon it was still looked upon as a creature worthy of a king and ruler.

The Red Dragon of Wales joined the ranks of the royal beasts when Henry VII ascended the throne in 1485. Claiming his descent from distant Cadwallader, Henry Tudor bequeathed the Red Dragon to his dynasty, whence it has passed through his daughter Margaret to the present Queen.

It was Edward VII who assigned the Red Dragon to the Prince of Wales as a token of his Principality in addition to the ostrich feathers which the Black Prince had won at the Battle of Crécy in 1346. In 1911 it was further decreed that the Princes of Wales should carry the red dragon on their princely shields and not simply on their badges, and this is the shield that is borne by Prince Charles today.

The Heraldic Antelope

The Heraldic Antelope is one of the best examples of the absurd lengths to which the old heralds allowed their scant knowledge of natural history to take them. The fierce beast of prey which they devised is so unlike the animal that we know, that is has always to be described as the Heraldic Antelope to avoid any ridiculous misunderstanding.

For all its gross inaccuracies though, the Heraldic Antelope is a marvellous confection. To the body of a stag are added the tail of a lion, the head of an heraldic tiger, tufts of hair on its tail, neck, chest and thighs, two serrated horns and a tusk growing from the tip of its nose.

Presumably it was regarded as a noble beast of prey, certainly the serrated horns were a fiercesome attribute. According to the writers of medieval bestiaries, they could be used to cut down trees.

The greatest popularity shown for the Heraldic Antelope in royal heraldry was by Henry IV, Henry V and Henry VI. These kings used the Heraldic Antelope as badges and it has been attributed to them as a supporter in conjunction with other beasts, notably the lion and the panther.

The Yale

Illustrations of the yale by medieval naturalists vary considerably but the one point on which they agree is the unique ability of the yale to twist its horns in any direction.

The yale inherited by the Queen resembles a goat with swivelling horns and tusks. This is the Beaufort yale, which was passed to the Queen's ancestor Henry VII, through his mother Lady Margaret Beaufort. This yale can be seen in St. George's Chapel, Windsor, as well as outside the two Cambridge colleges founded by Lady Margaret Beaufort, namely Christ's and St. John's.

Opposite page Queen Elizabeth made considerable use of the falcon as a heraldic beast. In this contemporary illustration she is actually using them to hunt

Above The phoenix was adopted as an emblem in the later years of Elizabeth's reign. This medal commemorates the Armada victory

Below The griffin, one of the earliest heraldic beasts, had the courage of a lion and the speed of an eagle

ILLVSTR. V.

The yale first appeared in heraldry on the arms of one of Henry IV's sons, John Duke of Bedford. It is likely that he regarded the yale as a hybrid of the Heraldic Antelope which had been borne by his mother and which was used by Henry V and Henry VI. The Duke of Bedford was also Earl of Kendal and some authorities believe that he punned the yale, or *eale* as it is called by Pliny, on Kendal, or Kend-eale. This earldom later found its way into the possession of Sir John Beaufort, who accordingly adopted the yale with the title. His daughter subsequently inherited the heraldic beast from her father and so it passed into the royal line.

The Griffin

The griffin is one of the oldest of the fabulous beasts of heraldry. Griffins have been found in archeological sites in many parts of the ancient Greek world and one golden model that was found in Crete was dated as being over 3,000 years old.

The griffin was regarded as sacred to the Sun. It was a beast of special significance and endowed with magical powers, so it was only right that it should combine the bodily attributes of the king of the birds, the eagle, with those of the king of the animals, the lion. In heraldry therefore the griffin is drawn with the head, neck, wings, and talons of an eagle, together with the hind quarters of a lion.

It also possessed the physical attributes of these two noble creatures. Griffins were believed to have the courage, boldness and strength of the lion as well as the speed and alertness of the eagle.

In two respects the griffin is closely allied with the unicorn. Like the unicorn it was believed to be fiercely independent, preferring death to captivity and like the unicorn, too, it possessed the power of detecting the presence of poison.

It was actually the claws and eggs of the griffin that were believed to change colour when they came into contact with poison and as a result of this miraculous power, they became as highly prized as the horn of the unicorn. They were both used as drinking vessels by those fortunate enough to possess them, though the supply of griffins claws was severely restricted, with only saints being allowed to claim them from griffins in payment for some special veterinary service. The cold light of science has revealed that griffins claws are in fact rhinoceros tusks and their giant eggs, the eggs of ostriches, but in the Middle Ages many kings felt proud and secure in the knowledge that their treasuries contained at least one of these 'essential relics' to royal survival.

The griffin is most closely associated in heraldry with Edward III who engraved it on his private seal.

The Phoenix

Like the dragon, the phoenix appears in oriental and western cultures alike. In China the phoenix is called 'Fum' or 'Fung' while in Japan its name is the unlikely 'Ho-ho'.

According to the ancient writers, the phoenix was the emblem of the souls of the departed that were enjoying eternal youth and never-ending pleasure in paradise. The traditional belief was that only one phoenix lived at any given time. This individual bird had a life-span of five hundred years, at the end of which it retired to some remote part of Arabia. There it built a fire of fragrant timber and sat on top of it. The fire was then lit by the intense heat of the sun and the phoenix was consumed only to be reborn from the ashes of the fire.

Left *The Lion of England is portrayed with characteristic French elegance. The display was mounted during the Queen's visit to Paris in 1972*

Above *Here an eastern dragon dances before Princess Margaret in a Hong Kong Schools Rally, 1966*

Below *Flags and banners being made especially for the Coronation, 1953*

monastic writers took to referring to Christ as 'the phoenix'.

The phoenix was used by Mary Queen of Scots as her badge in conjunction with the motto *'En ma fin est mon commencement'* ('In my end is my beginning'). This she took from her mother Mary of Lorraine.

Queen Jane Seymour also used the phoenix in flames on top of a castle as her badge and after her death in giving birth to Edward VI, the motto *'Nascatur ut alter'* ('That another may be born') was added to it. Her epitaph in St. George's Chapel, Windsor, reads:

'Here a phoenix lieth, whose death
To another phoenix gave birth.
It is to be lamented much
The world at once never knew two such.'

The Dukes of Somerset, the Seymours, still use the phoenix on their badge.

The phoenix seems to have been particularly favoured by Queen Elizabeth I. She used the bird as a symbol of her recovery from smallpox and it appeared on many medals and tokens struck during her reign accompanied by either her favourite motto *'semper eadem'* ('always the same'), or the less common *'sola phoenix omnis mundi'* ('sole phoenix of the world') which hailed the Queen as a phoenix in all but death.

It was only a matter of time before the early Christian writers transformed this legend into an allegory of the Resurrection, indeed later

M. KING EDWARD VII.
AND "CAESAR"

ROYAL ANIMAL MISCELLANY

*T*he royal family has become associated with certain animals by tradition and practice which do not fit into any easy classification but which nevertheless form an important element in the royal menagerie. And in this miscellaneous collection, birds and sea creatures play a significant part.

Swans have been considered as birds royal from time immemorial, due largely to the legend of the Swan Knight, Lohengrin. However, the first reference to the office of Royal Swan Keeper dates from 1295. Until the arrival of the turkey, the swan was an important game bird and a central dish in any large feast. Over the centuries nobility living near the river Thames were granted the privileges to take game for their consumption, though nowadays there are only three groups to whom this privilege is still extended, the

Vinters' Company, the Dyers' Company and the Crown.

The swans on the Thames are identified by a distinguishing mark made by cutting notches on the upper beak. However, the marking of royal swans was discontinued by Queen Alexandra, so today all the royal birds are unmarked. The swans belonging to the Vinters have a notch on either side of the upper beak, while the Dyers' swans have a notch on one side only.

This marking is done at the annual Swan Upping, which normally falls in the third week in July, the time when the cygnets which have to be marked are large enough to be handled. The jurisdiction of the Royal Swan Keeper lies between Blackfriars and Henley, and in that reach the Crown owns about five hundred swans, while the Dyers are allocated

sixty-five birds and the Vinters forty-five.

Further down the river, in the Tower of London, another group of birds, the famous ravens, watch over the survival of the Tower and the British Commonwealth. For according to a legend which dates from the time of Charles II, if ever the ravens leave, their departure will mark the fall of both.

In addition to these two groups of birds which may be regarded as 'permanent', certain members of the royal family are entitled to a variety of creatures that appear from time to time in British rivers and around the country's shores.

Any sturgeon caught in the country becomes the property of the Crown. Any whale washed ashore on the coast of Cornwall becomes the property of the Duke of Cornwall, Prince Charles. And any whales washed ashore within the area covered by the Cinque Ports of Hastings, Romney, Hythe, Dover and Sandwich are the responsibility of the Lord Warden of the Cinque Ports, at present the Queen Mother.

As Duke of Cornwall, Prince Charles also receives a number of amusing tributes from his tenants, most of which are waived today. According to time-honoured custom he is entitled to receive a tribute of puffins from the Isles of Scilly and from the people of north Cornwall, around Launceston, he can claim various hunting requisites, which include a bow and quiver of arrows, a grey cloak and two greyhounds.

Gifts of animals of another sort were willingly accepted by the royal family in the past and together they form a highly prized collection at Sandringham today. These are the stone carvings of animals made by the jeweller to the Tsars in the nineteenth century, Carl Fabergé.

The collection of carved animals originated, like almost everything else to do with the animal world at that time, with Queen Alexandra. The Queen was the sister of the Tsarina Marie and she had a very high regard for the work of Carl Fabergé, in particular his small animals and birds carved from semiprecious, coloured stones. So when a close friend of the royal family suggested that she might like to have some of her own animals carved by Fabergé both she and the King willingly accepted.

As the project developed, however, Edward VII became determined to have every animal on the estate carved, and he also made the stipulation that none of them were to be duplicated. Every animal given to the Queen was to be original and unique. For several months artists from Fabergé's studios made models of the King's pet terrier Caesar, his Derby winner Persimmon, the Queen's favourite dogs, as well as the cows and bulls, hens and cockerels, ducks, horses and pigs in the farmyards. These were then carefully scrutinised by the royal family in the dairy at Sandringham one December afternoon in 1907, and having been passed, were sent to St. Petersburg to be copied in stone.

More animals from the Fabergé collection at Sandringham

Here the animals' colourings were matched as closely as possible with a variety of semi-precious stones and the carvings were made to be as lifelike as possible. As an additional advantage they cost within the region of thirty pounds each, a sum which made them acceptable as presents from people who were not Her Majesty's closest friends.

The initial batch of Sandringham animals was a great success and commissions for hundreds of others followed, with the result that Queen Alexandra came to possess the most important collection of Fabergé animals outside Russia.

Among the three-hundred and forty-three models there are thirty-seven dogs, seven bears, twenty-two pigs and a litter of four piglets, forty-two elephants, ten monkeys, twenty frogs, two camels, twenty-two rabbits, two boars, a koala bear, a duckbilled platypus two shire horses, one of which is the Sandringham champion Field Marshall, two gnus, a sturgeon, a guinea-pig, a lioness, four rhinoceros, four seals and three bulls.

The tradition of presenting carved animals to the royal family is still as current today as it was a hundred years ago. Princess Anne's son, Peter Phillips, was presented with a complete toy zoo, carved by hand by Yootha Rose, the royal toymaker for thirty years who made his mother's first doll's house. 'I've decided on a zoo,' she explained, 'because small boys love them without fail.'

And if previous examples are anything to go by, it looks as if Peter Phillips is the first of yet another generation of royal animal lovers, breeders, conservers, hunters, and experts.

Acknowledgements

The photographs that appear on pages 10, 12 left, 15 below, 33 and 94/95 are
REPRODUCED BY GRACIOUS PERMISSION OF HER MAJESTY THE QUEEN

Other photographs are reproduced by kind permission of the following:

All Sport 50
Camera Press 22, 66 below, 90
Central Press 9 above, 13, 19, 43 below, 56, 57 above and below, 73, 77 right, 92 left
Cooper-Bridgeman Library 83
Fox Photos 8 above and below, 14, 23, 25, 48 above left, 60/61, 65 below, 74, 76 above right, 86/87 below
Robert Harding Associates 35
Keystone Press Agency 15 above, 51, 54, 55 above and below, 91 above
Serge Lemoine 4, 34 below, 47 above
Mansell Collection 12 right, 17, 52, 53 above, 73, 82 left and right, 86, 88, 89 above and below, 92 below, 93
John Moss 3, 47 below, 66 above, 71 above, 84 left and right, 85, 86/87 above
by courtesy of the Trustees, the National Gallery, London 38, 78
by courtesy of the National Portrait Gallery, London 34 above
Photographers International 18, 63
Popperfoto 16 below, 20, 21 above, 24, 28 left and right, 29, 32, 40 below, 41, 62, 68, 69, 70, 75, 76 left, 77 below, 91 below
Press Association 30
Radio Times Hulton Picture Library 6, 9 below, 16 above, 21 below, 24/25, 26, 26/27, 36, 37 left and right, 40 above, 44/45 above and below, 45, 53 below, 61, 64, 65 above, 76 below, 80, 81, 92 above right
Rex Features 42/43, 62/63 above and below, 71 below
Sport and General 48 above right and below
Syndication International 39, 43 above, 46, 58

Picture research by Leo Elford

Design by Albert Murfey